STARS In Our EYES

Photo by Baron Wolman

STARS In Our EYES

AN UNAUTHORIZED BIOGRAPHY

by Serena Czarnecki

BearManor Media

2021

Stars In Our Eyes: An unauthorized biography

© 2021 by Serena Czarnecki

All rights reserved.

No portion of this publication may be reproduced, stored, and/or copied electronically (except for academic use as a source), nor transmitted in any form or by any means without the prior written permission of the publisher and/or author.

Published in the United States of America by:

BearManor Media
1317 Edgewater Dr #110
Orlando FL 32804

bearmanorbare.com

Printed in the United States.

All photos used with permission.

Typesetting, cover, and layout by John Teehan

Back cover photo by Titus Moody

ISBN—978-1-62933-674-9

DEDICATION

For Jacub Bernard Antoni—
James Bernard Anthony Czarnecki

I will always be your little girl.

and

Special Thanks to Morgan

Table of Contents

1. Beginning 1
2. Mommy and Daddy 15
3. Aunts 37
4. Modeling 51
5. Film 57

Pictorial Interlude 79

6. First Husbands 95
7. Second Husbands 103
8. Third Husbands 115
9. Drugs & Drugs 127

Afterword 141

Chapter 1

Beginning

As I walked up the 140-plus stairs today, the cooing of birds accompanied me. My dad would call, "Bob-White, Bob-White" each morning, answering the birds where we lived in Southern California. This was special to me, the love of Nature bringing us ever closer.

Getting sun on my face now at the top of my climb, seeing Mt. Tamalpais, Mt. Diablo and the Bay (Today it's so clear that I see the snow-topped mountains of the Sierra Nevada!), I think of Daddy while listening to the birds. My favorite photograph of Daddy is of him sitting on a stone bench with white birds on his shoulders, lap, beside him.

At first I thought I'd write a one-woman play about her. I wanted to be her, play the role of her on stage. Now I am getting too old, she died so young. I have outlived her by decades, and happily. I didn't even meet my soul-mate until I was forty, and she passed away while still in her in her thirties. I've wondered what I can do with all of my collected research, spanning many notebooks. Should I attempt a biography? Perhaps a play? How should I approach her life? Through her eyes, through my own? I have finally come to the conclusion that a book about her isn't a story only of her life, but of my own love of her. Another adoring fan wanting to see her lovely smile.

Thank you to all who've told about her in books, interviews, magazine and newspaper articles, and the people I've met who knew her. My memory is filled with your stories of her as I write.

Throughout this time, I've drawn and continue to represent her image. She's come through my pencil and pastels, through the watery illusions of paint. I spend days with my focus on my paint box, paper, washes with photos of her surrounding the work space. She lifts my spirits, inspires my line.

Beginning

Never am I really happy in my images of her—yet I like my Art well enough to enjoy the pictures on their own merit; she was there in my consciousness at the moment creativity was ignited.

Once upon a time two Princesses were born thirty years apart. One would become a Sex Goddess throughout the world, the other a Priestess of Porn. Their lives would intermingle in various ways, as the Sex Goddess would affect many—even after her death. She'd continue to inspire lust and heartbreak to the public.

I've been reading and writing about her for years. I have loved The Actress since I was a little girl. Because I was a tow-head with a pouty mouth, people used to say I looked like her. My father had a pet name for her as I couldn't pronounce her name: "Sweetness."

Tim Leary, who I knew and visited at his home in Los Angeles, met Sweetness. He was just out of his Academic life, at a party in Hollywood. Sweetness wanted LSD. He explained it was not to use indiscriminately, but should be taken under scientific supervision. She found him at The Source Restaurant (a vegetarian place I went to in the

1970's) the next day and convinced him to give her a small dose. They did take a small amount that night and walked along the beach. Tim said it was "Joyful." I took a few trips until I had a bad one, then I stopped using the drug. The times I took LSD were extremely erotic and totally joyful. I still feel that I was blessed through this drug to have an "awakening"—secrets of the Universe were shown to me, and I was able to carry some of that wisdom back into my everyday existence. Those trips of long ago most assuredly affect my Art work.

My daughter's green eyes are astonishing. My sister has amazing blue eyes—blue-blue like my True Love's. I've never considered my eyes my best feature, they are blue/gray.

Sweetness's eyes were blue/gray, and she was expert at applying make-up. (So talented that a make-up person really wasn't necessary, she was so apt at application.) I am thankful for my eyes that help me create images for my canvasses, and see the beauty of our planet.

She was sensitive like me: if you raised your voice at her she might cry: I feel as though I'm being scolded. Even though I'm not a Perfectionist like she was, I get very upset if told I'm doing something wrong, I want to live in peace so badly. I'll pout, not speak; sit outside in the dirt in the dark—to punish myself. I overreact to "harsh words." I end up feeling that people are being mean to me; my Mania can kick in and it can torture me, or be violent.

Sweetness was an anxious person, my mom was also that type, and Mom had OCD because of her anxiety. I think some of Sweetness's "Perfectionism" was a sort of OCD due to Anxiety.

She was the first celebrity to come out in what is called the "Me-Too Movement." She was quoted saying that a Studio Head had assaulted her. I got "She's asking for it" a lot because no matter what I was wearing it was considered too sexy.

Sweetness was born with a gift not understood by anyone, least of all her! She had amazing comedic timing and an innate sense of how to play a scene, what roles didn't suit, and what to say to the press. She'd be persistent with Directors, and was usually right. Sweetness set high-standards for herself; if she wasn't perfect in a scene she would do it again until satisfied.

Another way we are connected: through a painting I see each day. It is of a couple who look identical to my mom and dad. Since they both have passed, seeing them in my mind means everything to me. My folks ended their days living in Oregon because they loved to walk in the rain together, they collected paintings and prints of others doing just that. Their idea of romance! In this painting in my living room the couple are wearing overcoats that resemble the ones my parents wore. They each had a closet full of coats and boots by their front door. I inherited this painting, and it's a joy seeing them on the wall and in my heart each day. The work is signed "Benay" and my Paul looked up the artist on a computer search. The woman painted, yes—but is widely known for her acting. She understudied the lead in *Annie Get Your Gun* on Broadway. The woman that played Annie on stage also did a movie with Sweetness. Perhaps an indirect connection, but strong as a spider's thread.

Serena and Sweetness were born California orchids: hothouse flowers wild at heart. Sweetness needed a group of people to tend her—her hair needs, make-up, clothes and to teach acting to her.

People to fawn over her and give her drugs. Ayn Rand would say that The Actress was a hero; that only a strong woman could be such a survivor and that is why the public loved her.

I accepted many people's help but have ended up living happily with one good man—mostly far from the spotlight. The author Ayn Rand changed my life, gave me the formation of my ideals, and wrote a tribute piece to Sweetness. I have read this woman writer's controversial words over and over, re-reading her books.

Sweetness, like me, never graduated high school, yet we both took college classes. I had two songs written for me. The first was a gag tune in a summer camp: "Serena, Serena you are the most! Serena, Serena I give you a toast!" at which point I was handed a burnt piece of bread. (Just as we later did while watching midnight showings of "Rocky Horror Picture Show.") A musician who played organ wrote a serious love song to me, which I heard when he gigged. He was in the band that had a major "hit" at the time—it was played at my junior high's dances and at wedding ceremonies across the land.

She had various songs written for her during and after her life. One song written for her was later changed into a Memorial song for a real-life Princess.

I have a white mole in the exact place that Sweetness penciled hers in on her cheek near her mouth. I've often been tempted to pencil mine in, but thought better of that, concerned that I'd be seen as copying her. However, in early modeling photos of The Actress, the mole is not to be seen, and when she first used a marker to show a mole it was on her chin!

My childhood was filled by dance lessons, acting lessons, performing in circle-in-the-round theatre. And singing lessons, which I was terrible at—couldn't keep a tune, had no voice, was flat and probably scratched my vocal cords. I was no more musical on an instrument—the guitar, even a tambourine—I just couldn't keep a beat. I loved to dance and would dance professionally, but only to striptease—my lack of musical ability hindered any real chance at a career in jazz, tap or modern ballet. Sweetness, however, sang in a lovely sweet breathy voice and could stay in key. She learned guitar for one film she was in, and ukulele for another; she'd played piano since she was a kid.

Though never receiving the biggest award from the acting community, Sweetness did go to ceremonies and did receive many Fan and Press-sponsored prizes and trophies. It was thirty years after I left the X-rated film business before the folks at AVN caught up to me! I was awarded their Hall of Fame Award in 2019. I went to Las Vegas to accept it at their convention, thanks to my dear friend the Colonel paying for flights. I enjoyed a spectacular birthday dinner cooked by my son-in-law and drank champagne and ate cheesecake with candles on it. Love him and my gorgeous daughter and the kids. (My three intelligent, gorgeous Grandkids!) Shortly before Sweetness died, she had champagne with a sheet cake for her birthday on the set of the film she would never complete. Staying with my sweet sister and her charming husband, they helped me get to the AVN venue and took great care of me. My sis and I attended a cocktail party where I was presented with a fabulous trophy that was made by the same company that makes the "Oscars"! It is absolutely gorgeous, the box in which it rests is gorgeous. I will always cherish receiving The Hall of Fame Award and consider it MY Oscar!

She received regular massages to sooth her. Sweetness used what she'd learned to massage the Washington DC official she dated to ease his back. One of the places known where he'd meet female companions was at the Carlyle Hotel in Manhattan. I stayed there once and was impressed by its old-world charm, and met Anthony Perkins in the lobby.

American Dream/American Tragedy.

Dream: rags to riches. Tragedy: drugs. Her mother was married while a pregnant teen; she was married a few times, had children, and beaten until she bled. Sweetness's grandmother also lived with abusive men. The reason her mother might have snapped was that she never got over her husband "kidnapping" her children, and she'd look for them all over the country. I've never forgiven my first husband for "stealing" my daughter. Even though she and I now have a lovely relationship, it took a lot of work on both our parts. We needed to learn to trust each other and our own feelings. Now I realize my first husband had his reason: my bipolar disorder was out of control.

BEGINNING

Like me, my daughter has been through marriages and has finally found "The One." My darling Paul and I attended their wedding on Arbor Day (and my rabbi's birthday.) The Rose Ceremony was beautiful, the reception afterwards a blast. Lucy's son never stopped dancing, a whirlwind. My granddaughter had grown up so much that I needed to be introduced! The food was delicious (I had three full platefuls) and the champagne kept flowing. I wish them a happy-ever-after.

Sweetness never found happiness with a partner, she belonged to nobody but her public.

Thank the goddess my Gemini mom had high-standards—though all the family is weird, we all turned out pretty good. My Gemini daughter raised herself without me, pulled up by her own high-standards. (She is such a good Mom and finally my good friend.)

Sweetness constructed an act with baby-talk and being weak. Her show of helplessness was attractive to all those big, strong men! Her life consisted of ways to win favor from people, to get what she wanted and needed, to win love and favor. Sweetness was born under the sign of Gemini.

Sweetness was given to foster parents when only two weeks old. Sweetness had bad luck, she lacked a caring parent. Bad luck in husbands: men she couldn't meld with, no children but terrible pain in her womb that would remind her of being childless. "Friends" who would feed her drugs—barbiturates being so new on the market they weren't understood. When I think of her, she reminds me to appreciate what I have, how I can be of help, grateful for all I've been given. Her life demonstrates all one needs to be really happy: to be loved and to love.

I've been watching her movies over again—again, again! No matter what else is going on, who else might be saying lines, it is only her I see. I can't keep my eyes off her! When she exits the scene I feel let down, needing more, more. She was one of a kind. Many women would copy her, none could replace her. Fame would continue to grow as the years passed. She would go from a girl to a woman from model to Actress, from a Star to a Legend, into the realm of myth. Goddess-like.

A book called *Golden Goddesses* has a chapter about me—I was a Star in the Golden Age of Erotica.

Beginning

My mom "grew me up" to be an Artist. Van Gogh was my example. She loved his work, and so I love his paintings. He was crazy—but I was able to be treated, finally, with medications. I have hurt my body severely, even breaking bones, but never cut off an ear! I admire how much Vincent believed in himself; he kept painting through all, kept painting though never selling a painting. I admire his lust to create.

Mom was also a huge movie buff. Her father would paint the posters for movies before they were mass-printed. She loved Garbo, he painted Garbo. We feel that we were close to films. Mom would go on to work for a Studio. My mom could remember every "character" actor's name, the plot as well as the Stars of every film from her youth.

Sometimes when high on weed, or in my night dreams, I "become" the Actress. I feel as she must have, and soon it becomes too much, too sad for me to process. I had such a great connection with my folks, they were the two people in the whole damn world I knew would always care for me when I was in trouble or in pain. My parents would take me into their home and heal me, speak with me, take me out for meals and entertainment.

Sweetness's mom was in her own world and would ignore the child, leave her to others to be raised. Her father completely denied her very existence.

Chapter 2

Mommy and Daddy

LIFE BEGINS WITH YOUR MOTHER, the bond between mother and child the strongest of all. Sweetness never had that foundation for her life as her mother was "absent." She never knew her father, looked for him her entire life. Thought she found him, but the man she approached rejected her, didn't want anything to do with her. She looked for her father figure in the men she married.

I was a "Daddy's Girl" on the other hand. Me and my dad did everything together, loved each other, loved each other's company. We would sing at the top of our lungs to the radio as he drove, go to the parks and the wild places to photograph, see everything that was free of charge, tour around neighboring towns on Sundays. I loved my dad completely, and I was greedy taking all of Mom's affection. Dad and I melded immediately. Mom loved me unconditionally, she was my fiercest champion.

I've read books and books about The Actress's life, jotting down notes. The man she assumed was her father may not have been, who knows? Maybe that is the truth of why he rejected her; her mother was so mixed up—*she* may not have known the truth, and he was easy prey. There is mystery surrounding Sweetness's birth, which would confuse the girl all her life—not knowing a fact digs one more hole in a person's outlook. Her mother would use different last names, the girl's name also being changed—there seemed no true anchor (except her own sheer Will) in her life. There was mystery regarding her birth, and mystery surrounding her death.

I was at my Daddy's side in the hospital to see the heartbeat machine flat-line. I was the only one there, the rest of the family taking a needed break from their constant vigilance. It is a moment I treasure, feeling that our spirits were one, seeing him off to a place of no pain. Daddy suffered for years, probably a slave to all the painkillers he took, underwent so much. Put up with my rebellion as well as many surgeries and so much pain. I am deeply honored to have spent his last moments on this earth with him: he saw my birth, I saw his death. I hope that he and Mom are now on a second honeymoon way out yonder of the Earth's Moon!

She, ever the loving wife, had "the incident" that killed her on his birthday. My family was sure this was a sign she was ready to go to him. She'd been living with my younger sister. My other sister and I watched Mom's collapse, and our brother (Mom's only boy) stayed with her until she went to Dad.

Even though my bipolar disorder would cause torment for my entire family, I was always welcomed in to their hearts, never once rejected. And oh, how I tried to be awful, screaming and flinging myself in "tantrums." My mom was tolerant of my mental breakdowns, very patient—but I realize now how I must have hurt her. I was out of control, out of my mind. My hope, now that I've leveled out with medication, is that they knew how thankful I was, and am, to have them as parents. I love them very much. Daddy's Girl could never repay him with enough Love.

To be without Love from your father is a tragedy in Sweetness's life, a rejection harsher than any the Studio could hand out.

My own childhood was full of fun with my dad. We'd go places especially to take pictures of me, sing songs together. I can't sing a lick, but joyously do it at the top of my lungs. Dad had a pleasant voice, a fantastic whistle, and good Daddy Hugs. I lived to make him smile at my antics. She never knew a father and was handicapped in life because of that. To be missing such a huge chunk of one's development (the very forming of a Person's Hopes and Ideals)—how horrid an emptiness, how blank a place that needed nourishment.

She was quite well-read. I get my love of reading from my mom, who always had a stack of books she was reading next to her bed. I'd raid the bookshelves as a kid and got in contests at school, winning prizes (that were books) for reading many books. I read all the Tarzan books which were on the family shelves, then science fiction, then discovered Agatha Christie which led to years of reading mystery novels.

Finally I found autobiographies and bios to have all the richness that only real-life can offer. By reading peoples' stories, a sense of the time they lived in and their circumstances might be rendered. Life is stranger than fiction.

The Actress had a hero: Abraham Lincoln. My heroes: Serena Williams 'cause she's tough, Hillary Clinton who I voted for (thank you for your fight for the mentally ill) and Ruth Bader Ginsburg (thank you for showing us Justice, and a great love affair), Michelle Obama and her husband the President (for everything), Gloria Steinem for getting the word out!

My life happy, while she grew up between caretakers and in an orphanage. My laughter was genuine, she would smile for the cameras. There was nothing for me to worry over as a child, not a care. I thought how much fun I could have: I decided whether I'd be an Indian or a Cowgirl that day, would I shoot a bow and arrows or my cap pistol. I visited the neighbors and played with the children on the block, had a lively Social System. I was usually the Leader of our games which consisted of Pretend sessions. Each day I designed a fort or forest; the whys and wherefores of the all-important story: the struggle. I'd exhaust myself play-fighting: shooting, hiding, running, climbing trees.

In elementary school I saw a great deal of my dad, as he'd been hurt at work and underwent many surgeries. He was in casts, on crutches and at home. The baby was still a baby, I was Daddy's Girl. And also being a really good student, a Teacher's Pet. The waking of my hormones in Middle School, the budding of my Sexuality, I welcomed attention from boys my age—none of whom Daddy liked. Natch.

Mother was the rock of our family, all us kids relied on her wisdom and caring, whereas Sweetness's mother was slightly off-kilter. Due to her circumstances, her mother would go deeper into insanity the older she got. Her mother never recovered from having her children taken away; my mom kept us all close through two marriages. My dad was the love of my mom's life, but Sweetness would marry three times, never finding her soul-mate, her One True One.

Although I too married several times, I did finally meet the man of my deepest love dreams. He has been there for me in everything I attempt, been loving and supportive. He is everything I could ever hope for in a partner—a lover, a friend, a kind, caring person. And so handsome! (Cutest thing I've ever seen!)

Her mother was diagnosed with paranoid schizophrenia. My legally-blind aunt had schizophrenia, and at the end of her life was kicked out of Homes because she'd take off her clothes and run nude down the street. Sweetness's Mom had hallucinations, and thought men were coming to kill her. Sweetness's grandmother died in a straitjacket in a mental hospital; "craziness" was in the blood. When Sweetness saw her mother, having seen her only one time in eleven years, it is unclear if her mother knew how ill she really was, she wore a nurse's uniform! Did she understand that she was a patient in the hospitals in which she stayed?

Both The Actress's mother and my mom worked for Studios on the sidelines of film making. Sweetness and I would find our "home" in front of the camera. She'd want more from her "home" and the silver screen was merely my temporary "home". I am at home with my Paul—wherever he goes, I will follow.

She was born to a Flapper in the boom times of the Roaring Twenties. Women had the Vote for the first time thanks to the first wave of Feminism. I was born in the conservative 1950's but spent my formative years in the Hippy Era of Free Love. She lived until the 1960's, the beginning of the next wave of Feminism. What I have done in my life was due to my Feminist outlook.

The worst times for the famous Actress were in her childhood foster care and the orphan's home. She says that she had only one change of clothes and no one came to visit her. She felt so alone. I remember having so much fun with my mom when she'd take me shopping for a new wardrobe each school year. We'd go to the town of Montrose where the shops were, spend hours trying on and selecting clothes for class and after-school rump-around togs. She'd always buy me and my sister garments just for Easter (with bonnets), pretty red and green dresses for Christmas, too. This time we spent together were hours of happiness. On these shopping days we'd stop at a coffee shop, sit at the counter, and have a treat—always a freshly-baked bran muffin and black coffee for Mom, I'd get a blueberry muffin with a glass of cold milk. (It was the only time I ever sat at a counter, so that made it even more memorable.)

Love for the girl was unknown, unresolved. She grew up with a deep need for Love. She wanted something that was huge and vague because she'd never had it, never felt its completeness. She would rely on the Love of her Public. Fickle though fans might be, she was worshiped by both men and women—those who lusted and those who wanted to save her.

Growing up, Sweetness was placed in many foster homes. In one she was molested, but her foster mother slapped her when told about it. A boarder in the house invited the little girl into his room, then locked the door and made her promise not to tell. I too was molested—by a family member—when I was a preteen. I didn't tell anyone, but my younger sister knew because she saw me right afterward. My sister has never forgiven him; it took me years to even talk to him. Eventually I needed to forgive him for the sake of my Soul. I want to rid my psyche of the dirt of jealousy, greed, and the muddled waters of fear and hate.

Her mother had a son that died and she would have paranoid hallucinations about the boy. In the Depression Era she had another child to raise, Sweetness, but she just was unable to cope. The slightest noise that Sweetness would make could disturb her, set her off. Between ear operations, my mom was acutely sensitive to sound and the entire family walked on pins and needles—finally her hearing was balanced and we all could breathe again, speak in normal voices again. Unfortunately Mom, due to her deafness, never was interested in music, whereas Dad hung out with musicians in his youth.

Sweetness and I both caught Whooping Cough, unusual in my day as most kids got vaccinated. I know children should get vaccinated (in order to protect everyone) but my mother was scared of doctors because her mother was scared of doctors. My grandmother (Busha) only took one aspirin in her life!

Sweetness and her mother were both born under the astrological sign of Gemini, The Twins. I was born between two Geminis: my mother and my daughter.

Her mother broke Sweetness's heart because while she did remember happy times with her mom, her mom could not care for her. Her mom had to be taken care of. Her mother made sure to pay the foster parents for her board, and would visit. Her first foster parents had other foster kids, and loved them all dearly—no matter what publicity would come out later. Sweetness would spin a woe-is-me tale about her upbringing—but not all was painful and lonely.

Her heart was broken by the man she thought was her father. Sweetness was told that she was a "Love Child," the polite way to say "bastard"—that her mother wanted to marry the man but he didn't want to have anything to do with mother or baby. He was a "Player" as they say. Her mother first named her last ex-husband as the child's father on the birth certificate, then changed that to the name of her first husband! No wonder Sweetness was confused, even her mother really wasn't sure of the father. Her mother was dating several men while working with her friend, the honorary Aunt. The aunt and her mom were having quite a time going out and having fun. They dated fellow workers, and her mom thought it was her boss at the Studio that impregnated her.

Her mother and honorary Aunt were both flappers in the 1920's, and her mother knew she couldn't take care of another child. Sweetness was given up to foster parents when still a tiny baby. She says that for twelve years she was unhappy and rarely saw her mother, but the foster parents said that in actuality Sweetness was a happy child and they loved her dearly. Another misconception she fed to the Public.

Sweetness was quite apt at spinning tales to suit her image. She did live in several households and an orphanage, but it seems she was less than truthful about her care. The stories she'd tell of her unhappy childhood would endear her to her public, but much of what she said seems to be twisted to her advantage, some fabrication mixed with reality.

Sweetness says she washed a lot of dishes and scrubbed floors as a kid. I got an allowance when, as a preteen, I was asked to do one chore weekly. For my money I was to sweep the driveway—that's it! But I hated every minute of this "torture"! Sweetness says she was the last one in the bath in Care, and the water would be cold and dirty. As an adult she'd stay in a hot bubble bath all day long.

She was told never to call her foster parents Mom or Dad, so she felt she had no parents. Even though her own mother was alive, she was strange to the girl. The one person that touched her, hugging her and curled her hair, was her "Aunt," best friend of her mother's. Her mother and her "Aunt" worked together at a Movie Studio—cutting film. They were great friends and shared the same dress and shoe size—both were five feet tall. They'd swap clothes all the time, went out on the town as "Flappers."

I remember trading clothes with my friend in junior high. Clothes are everything at that age—clothes and how you wore your hair, how long was the boy's hair. I wore the extremes: micro-mini skirt with my underwear showing, or floor-touching flowing skirts and hiking boots. Bell-bottoms—I'd add fabric to jeans to make the bottoms even wider, cut jeans in half and make skirts out of them. Many patches on the jeans, embroidery, ripped hems by walking on them. Stylin'.

As a baby, The Actress didn't have a crib. Her mother pulled out a dresser drawer and that's where she slept. I remember my baby sister napping in a drawer, and Mom would bathe us in the kitchen sink until we were toddlers. I recall Sis in her crib from a couple of homes where we lived; once Mom rushed in to move it when she had a hunch—and sure enough, the wall caved in from a flood right where the crib had sat. Always follow your hunches.

Her father wouldn't see her, wouldn't take responsibility for her ever—even after Sweetness was famous. He owned a dairy farm and she went there twice. He turned her away both times. A picture of him was on her mother's wall, and the little girl wished he'd love her; he looked like a famous actor to her—someone she would eventually act in a movie with. Her "father" didn't want her, and her mother couldn't take care of her. I, on the other hand was blessed into middle-class white America in a prosperous time. (Remember? There used to be a middle class.) Dad never saw color, so I was raised with his many black friends. My favorite field trip with my folks was going to Watts to visit the marvelous Towers. Truly inspiring. We were the perfect nuclear family in many ways: we'd all gather after work/school for family dinner. While my mother worked, when most mothers stayed home like "good housewives," I was not a latch-key kid. Mother must have gone through scheduling changes to always be there when her family needed her. We needed her every day for all the give and take of parent/child relations. We needed her to hand us our prepared lunch, or money for the cafeteria. We needed her kissing our scuffed knees. We all depended on her love—no matter what. (And, oh! I tested that Love, I stretched it but it held strong. I know without any doubt that my mother loved me. Being an un-diagnosed bipolar person can break even the strongest love, but not Mom's for me.)

The doctor at the institution into which her mother was put said that her brain was only half the size of a normal person's. My father's heart was extra small the doctor told me when Dad lay dying. To me, to the family, he had a heart as big as Forever, as big as the great state of Texas. A heart enormous with tenderness and much fortitude. He was a brave man—when fighting in WWII, then to take up a family not his own. He was successful as a father and as a man, "all that and a bag of chips." Dad endured surgery after surgery on his knee, hip and heart.

Her mother just couldn't cope, if she got over-worried she'd break down. My mother was extremely level-headed yet would worry all the time over her children. One time when Sweetness lived with her mother they had only one piece of furniture: a white piano. The girl was in the kitchen one day when she heard her mother in the other room laughing and screaming: Making a lot of noise, screaming and laughing hysterically. Throwing things, screaming and laughing. An ambulance took her mother away that day. Her mother said the white piano had been owned by a very famous actor, but it was sold off after she was taken to the hospital. Sweetness found it and bought it when she had modeling money, and the grand piano was re-furbished and once again played. Nowadays pianos are becoming a thing of the past because people don't have room for them, but having a piano in the home is like capturing the magic of music. Times were that folks would entertain themselves with piano recitals and standing around the piano singing together.

I was taken away by ambulance to mental wards in three counties. I've felt the binding of a straight-jacket, the loneliness of a padded room, the distrust of other patients, the disdain for the doctors.

When I had "Tizzies" as my Mom called them, I'd scream. Scream until my throat was sore; cry and throw anything I laid my hands upon. In the early days living with my True Love, I was still acting-out: screaming and banging my head against the wall. Pain was a comfort to me when others wouldn't get close. Her mother went to several hospitals for the rest of her life, but never seemed to understand that she was sick. She thought she was a nurse and would return to her job cutting film. I can relate. I didn't realize I was sick, either. But through many scenes and tantrums and tears I finally got a notion that I wasn't acting quite like others and found my way to help and medication. Thank goodness! Being mentally healthy has kept me alive. But being in that altered existence, one doesn't know any other life, everything seems normal—even though you are breaking your bones, cutting yourself, and smashing glasses against the wall. I wouldn't accept that I was "sick" until late in my twenties.

Sweetness's mother was just "the redheaded lady" to her. My mother, too, was a red-head. Mom had rich, thick beautiful auburn-colored locks. As a young woman working in Hollywood for the Studio System—it's a Company Town—Mom realized she couldn't act, and that her exquisite hair color could be had out of a box. So my mom took stock of her talents, and realized she could become an Observer, a Patron, the one who appreciates. (All artists depend on these people.) All of Mom's kids have some of her strong red hair color, I'm what they call a Strawberry Blonde. Yum, yum! I always liked that term!

Sweetness watched her mother slide into insanity, and it was terrifying to the girl. When released from the hospital her mother began wearing the white uniform of a nurse. The child didn't understand it, but her mother actually found work in convalescent hospitals!

My redheaded mother bundled up at the beach to protect her fair skin from the sun. I would also freckle and burn with too much sun. How gorgeous my mother's hair was: dark auburn and thick, wavy. How rich the color, Mom didn't turn white until quite aged. My mother gave all her kids a bit of Irish color, mixed with our dad's Polish blonde. One sister has red hair, my brother is blonde with a red beard, my other sister reddish/brownish/blonde. I am reddish blonde. We all grew up interesting and beautiful thanks to our Mom and Dad. We were taught that Artist is a fine vocation, an Art Appreciator also good. Dad would always brag how artistic Poles are.

A woman prayed with The Actress's mother and got her interested in Christian Science. My father was in a Christian Science hospital one time, a contradiction of terms! He heard horror stories of what the followers believed in, health wise. No one—her mother's friends' prayers or the doctors—could seem to help her mother's condition. Much prayer would be said over her, and also for Sweetness, who would grow up also having dark moods.

I have had to deal with the ups and downs of being bipolar: being so manic so that I can't sleep for days, being so depressed that I'd crawl under the covers and sleep for days. I've thought of killing myself numerous times, usually not taking myself too seriously! I made half-hearted attempts for attention, but did throw myself off a mountain when I could not cope.

Sweetness was suspicious of life, always expecting the worst to come her way. My mother the Gemini was diagnosed with anxiety, and had OCD—getting along quite well, though. Mom was raised by a loving mother, my Busha, and even in Mom's teens they loved to hang out together. Busha spent most of my life in our family home.

Sweetness worried. My family called Mom a "Worry-Wart." (Still no idea what this means, we musta said it because it was funny.) Sweetness worried about being abandoned and hurt; Mom just worried as a part of her nature. Mom worried about her brood. Sweetness pushed for different roles because she worried about being "aged out" like actors known for their sex appeal are. Every actress comes to an age when getting work becomes difficult. A valid point: Actresses over a certain age have a difficult time in Hollywood, especially when seen only as pretty and sexy. Sweetness wished for serious roles to be given to her. She'd fallen in love with the art of acting, and hoped to continue to act later in life. My mom taught me to love acting as an observer. I love many people's acting, including Sweetness's, of course.

Sweetness was a sad and lonely little girl. I was a happy child made lonely by bipolar disease. I wasn't at ease with my out-of-control mania, my deep, black depression. I've always depended on the kindness of men, my lovers. I could never keep a woman friend. I've come to accept this: now my best friend is a producer of wonder, and a bipolar. We are able to cut to the root of things because we can feel how the other thinks. He is a creative genius and produces books and videos and music. Many of my other friends are people I've never met but know through the internet. My childhood friend Leah I always call my Best Friend, though I see her once every twenty years.

When her mother was in the hospital for the mentally-challenged, she said to Sweetness that she didn't remember giving birth to her. My birth was sudden; I couldn't wait to join the world and was early. My birth involved the entire family. Mom and I were on the way to Glendale Hospital when I decided it was time. My father and brother delivered me. My sister was at the baby shower. Dad commemorated the oak tree under which I was born with a silver plaque.

Sweetness wanted children, but not as a single parent; she was firm in her belief that a child needed two parents. After my daughter was taken from me I cried for years, every day. When I found somebody I wanted to have a child with, we tried. I'd been hurting with endometriosis since my periods began, so went to doctors hoping they'd help with the process of pregnancy. But when a tube-test was performed on me, putting ink through my ovarian tubes, I fainted in pain on the table. My tubes were blocked with scar tissue, there was no hope of getting pregnant another time.

Sweetness grew up not having her Mother present, I was for years without a daughter.

Chapter 3

Aunts

MY AUNTIE LUKE was highly artistic—full of tight hugs for me, and lots of laughs and love. She was actually my Godmother through the Catholic faith. I'd run bare-chested (pretending I was an Indian) to her home nearly every day as a small child. As an adult I'd see her with my folks to have Irish Coffee at San Francisco's famous Yerba Buena Restaurant. And she visited me with Busha at my decrepit three-story mansion, and create a pen and ink drawing of the occasion. My "real" Aunt Diane was married to my mother's brother, the fireman. She was a black-haired beauty, looked like a porcelain doll. She seemed be cool towards me, but she is the mother to my favorite cousin Robin. (We even look alike, talk alike.)

Her "Aunt" styled Sweetness after a long-ago Movie Idol and pierced the young teen's ears with a needle. I had my ears done by a classmate—on a sleep-over, she stuck a needle through my ears with a potato in back holding it all steady. They got infected, scabbed with puss and blood for weeks, and although they tore, my ears were proudly pierced, much to my mother's horror. Mom had numerous sets of earrings to match her necklaces to match her outfits which matched her shoes and coats—but hated piercings. When using drugs, I'd end up piercing my own right ear six or seven times, my left three times. Once I sobered up in my life I let all my skin heal, grow back together and I've never since wore earrings. (Although in a manic fit I had my eyebrow pierced for a short time. It went with my black crew-cut!) Lost some of my "Slave to Fashion" attitude as I've matured and found out what is really real: that I should strive for inner peace, and being loved is everything.

When Aunt lived with the future Actress and her mom they'd all go to the movies together and saw the beautiful movie palaces. This was much different than when the girl had lived with foster parents, who'd told her that watching a movie was a sin. The girl never saw them after she left their care, imagining herself a "sinner" in their eyes. While movie theaters weren't "Palaces" by the time I came around, they weren't Multiplexes either. A double-feature is what played; the floors were sticky, the popcorn stale, heated by a lamp but with lots of greasy fake-butter oil. You could stay through more than one showing if you had a mind to, and there were uniformed ushers with flashlights to seat you and tell you to shut-up.

Her "Aunt" told everyone at the Studio where she worked that Sweetness was the next Big Deal—she'd be a Movie Star. She'd take the girl to work with her and show her off in the nice dresses Aunt would buy. She'd have the child's hair curled and put ribbons in it. Stage plays were the thing for me! I saw a few amateur productions in little theatres and at Glendale College and was hooked. I appeared in plays at movie theaters and Center Theatre, at the YMCA, even at hospitals. During one stage show Mom curled my hair with rags in order to get perfect ringlets for the Period-Piece.

I had a blast also attending acting lessons and dance lessons. My wild-child energy was consumed in play-acting, pretend. Still the call of Drama would visit times at home where I had to "act-out" as they say. I was an uneasy child, impatient for more, more. I was hungry for the knowledge that living could give to me. Dad or Mom took me everywhere, which is now difficult to imagine, as Mom hated to drive, was extraordinarily nervous in an automobile. When I drove Mom I asked her to please sit in the back seat, but then she was *really* a back-seat driver!

Her aunt wanted the child to be just like her own favorite female Screen Idol. Sweetness wanted to please her Aunt who groomed her, and held her close. So the little girl wanted to be just like the dead movie star. The Aunt's Actress Idol died very young, at the top of her fame. Sweetness began to have dreams of being up there on the silver screen, famous, beautiful, loved by many—just like Auntie's Idol. I wonder if she knew she too would die young?

Her mom ended up giving her child to the "Aunt" to raise. Sweetness had already been in a number of foster families, then her Aunt ended up putting her in an orphanage. Sweetness begged and cried to her Aunt—she didn't want to go into the orphanage, she wasn't an orphan! But the girl's mother needed a mental rest and so she was put into the place she'd stay for years. Her heart was broken when she was dragged into the orphanage. While kids there would try to make her laugh, she was shattered, she knew she didn't belong there—had been put there only for the adult's convenience. While she would forgive, she would never forget her time in the institution.

Sweetness had another "Aunt" who was a Christian Scientist and they went to services twice on Sunday and once during the week. When she started having the horrible pain of menstrual cramps her Christian Scientist Aunt could do nothing for her, would not give her any medicines. She was a believer in not believing in medicine or doctors. She would have the girl kneel with her and pray. They'd pray aloud together and wait for the terror to pass. Aunt's Movie Idol died at 26 years old—as she lay dying her mother refused treatment because of her "religion." Sweetness would suffer with severe endometriosis her whole life.

Being tortured by excruciating pelvic pain in my teens I yelled and cried and could not explain my agony. I was put in several mental institutions, beginning when I was thirteen. My direct route to the straight-jacket was the unbearable pain (which I was unable to describe) in my uterus. One time, a cyst on my right ovarian tube became so large I looked like a pregnant woman; I was put into San Francisco General Hospital for a month-long antibiotic drip. It was written into her movie contracts that Sweetness couldn't work during that time of month, it was such torture. Sweetness would lie down, screaming and in pain. She had surgeries to help the pain, they didn't work. I would suffer with this as well, screaming nearly every month in pain. Finally endometriosis turned precancerous, and I had all my insides removed by surgery.

When endometriosis came to make my menstrual periods an agony, I was incorrectly diagnosed with PMS. In several mental institutions, in Los Angeles and in Camarillo, California, I was misdiagnosed. No one could know my pain, I was too scared to speak, unable to describe my hurt. It was big and dark and highly intimate and could overpower me. The rage I felt as a crimson fire-ball blazed in my solar plexus. I'd crawl under tables, hands over my ears, eyes clamped shut to avoid speaking with counselors.

Sweetness spent most of her time at home in her bathrobe. I sleep and live in a nightgown and a robe because it's chilly here in our forest, and the cabin isn't insulated. She thought nothing of being naked, didn't hide her body. Because of my bipolar disease I flaunted my nakedness to become a Star in erotic films and cover-girl/center-fold of sexy magazines. But when I was in my shopping phase of my manic disorder, I would try on outfit after outfit in dressing rooms. Sweetness had the luxury of playing different roles as an Actress. Faster and faster I spent, on a carousel of madness, getting to know the sales people in stores all over the county. I really thought they were my only friends. With each change of clothing I'd take on the personality of the person that might wear such a dress. The glittering of my Soul wanted to explore each facet of my Personality. In the reflection of many dressing-room mirrors I saw individuals dressed in costumes, many I brought home. But I wouldn't wear these lovely dresses and suits. I'd live in jeans, a t-shirt or the ever-present nightgown. But in the act of deciding upon which character I'd like to be (in the privacy of the room made for stripping and trying on clothes, a secure room with a mirror and the quiet of the store) I was full with creation. Within the space of one second I could turn my inner eye to each wave of emotion that I'd feel, fully experiencing deep depths of thought. I'd see myself reacting to various situations in the guise of whoever I became in each change of outfit. I was playing "dress-up." I played out each role that the new outfit would suggest to my ego. I'd spend hours in these minutes, giving the store some money for the privilege of my experience. I didn't need the clothes I would take away, I'd already had my experience, I didn't need to repeat it, I'd always be needing new things to entertain my time. The mania wouldn't allow me to rest, until the time I would crash.

The orphanage placed her with nine different families before she was married the first time. A woman came weekly to inspect the bottoms of Sweetness' shoes—if they had no holes in the soles, she'd report that the child was well taken care of.

The orphanage must have felt like a jail to her—always having to do what others told you to do, your privileges given and taken away. I have been in jail, it's horrible—it's meant to be! The very worst thing is the cold. Jail air and the benches you sit upon are freezing. It chills you to the bone; many hot, hot baths are needed afterward. No matter how many layers of clothing you are wearing, the jail cold will seep in and you shake not only from fright. I have also been in mental wards, like Sweetness's mother, and like she herself was once put in—you are convinced you don't need to be there with all those other really crazy people! (These institutions are also very cold.) There was mental illness in her family. Her grandfather died in an institution, but his "craziness" is said to have been caused by a venereal disease. But his wife, Sweetness's grandmother, was diagnosed with bipolar disorder and also died in a Home.

She developed early and looked older than she was—one of the reasons she was married off so young. I also looked older than my age and was in magazines and movies while still underage. For most of the first eight years of her life she was in foster care, but it was with a couple who fostered many kids and loved them. They were religious, and this led to the publicity about them, and that hurt their feelings. They really loved the child, and her mother did visit, which only confused the child. But she played with the foster children, and was taught piano, something she loved and was proud of for the rest of her life.

Sweetness was the first celebrity to speak publicly about sexual abuse. This was huge—way before the time of computers, cell phones, talk shows and "tell-alls" in which famous folks could speak of their drug-taking and sexual doings. Such things weren't talked about in those conservative days. Anything intimate was to be stamped down, kept inside, forgotten. It's been shown that numerous boys and girls then and now are abused. Sweetness never said she was raped, "just" molested. She may have felt unwanted pleasure, which could account for later guilt. Many victims of molesters are confused and can blame themselves. Because of their childhood trauma, they can be insecure about all relationships.

Even in elementary school Sweetness made up stories. Once she told a teacher that she saw her foster mother put one of the kids into the oven! Telling tales would continue to be her way of gaining sympathy and attention. My dad would tell long stories that would start in the middle, most of which the family thought were fibs, many of them we found to be true after he passed. My sister also has the gift of gab. I have never been confident except when given lines, so I exaggerate. If I say a million of them, you can rest assured, there might be a hundred!

Sweetness was teased by other kids that her mom was crazy, and ended up developing a stutter. I was teased for various things, but I have held back from getting close to people because of my illness. Mania and depression drove nearly everyone but my family away. That is why I've always needed a man to protect me. I figured he might stick by me through the tantrums, because when normal I could take care of his sexual needs. My agent, Bill Margold, knew I needed protecting—at first it was from fighting with, being verbally abused by, my first husband. It was also because I retract into solitude and fear coming out into the world. When Margold sent me to New York City (to get me away from first husband) I found my lover Jamie Gillis and we made movies together. I also found another Bill to take care of me on the Upper West Side. He was a piano player and wrote a song about me, and allowed me to crash at his apartment.

Since I've left the business, the business has provided me with friends among the fans. People have helped me and I've met folks I never would have being sheltered. Of the friends I've kept many are in loving, lasting marriages. Through another top porn star/radio talk-show host I met my third Bill. My "new" Bill's been a dear friend and has helped with hotels and airfare when I was in need. My new Bill knew Bill Margold, and took the torch of protecting me in hand. I've become an honorary Auntie to people I first met through the X-rated biz. I can, through the wonders of the computer, enjoy friends around the world. The editor of one of my books lives in Denmark and is a writer, artist and art critic. We've yet to meet, hoping that day will come for us—for now we email and are very close. What we'd love most is to be able to exhibit our artwork together.

Aunt helped her to answer fan mail.

At first Sweetness and her favorite Aunt would sign and answer the fan mail. But as more and more letters poured in as she became more famous she could not answer her mail because the shrinks would want her at her appointments. I think they needed her more than she needed them.

Chapter 4

Modeling

SWEETNESS WAS NOT TRULY A BEAUTY before surgery—facial re-construction. But she was enthusiastic and had a freshness about her. Her unruly curly hair would be lightened and straightened. Early modeling showed her as the "Girl Next Door." I've never been considered beautiful—my ears stick out—I've been called, "What Me Worry?" because of my ears. (When being cast in the film *10* John Derek said I was funny-looking.) I do love to pose, my agent used to say that I'd come alive in front of the camera lens. My daddy made me into a model.

Modeling for the still camera she flirted with the lens. She'd vamp, giggle, squeal in delight as the camera clicked. She had a wonderful time romping, showing off in the photographer's Studio. Loved when she could sip sherry and dance to music while getting photographed. Sweetness portrayed a gorgeous, sexy woman who is "available." Her sex appeal was touted as Hollywood's best glamour since the Movie Idol she patterned herself after. Modeling was the best part of my career, I loved to pose and be paid for being beautiful. We both use photo modeling as a way to achieve attention, success, a way to see what was happening in the great big world.

When Dad and I would go out together we'd go to beautiful parks all over LA County to photograph. He'd worked at a camera store and was a gifted amateur, encouraging my brother to become a professional photographer. I would act as his model. I love to pose—as seen in many magazine layouts later in my life. Posing, smiling for Daddy's camera I was a natural-born "ham." I couldn't get enough film! We both had fun under oak trees in the park, doing what we loved, taking pictures. (In my life with my True Love we've also lived in the trees, a redwood forest in Northern California. I even wrote a book of Love Poems to my Darling,

Modeling

and to the trees and the mountain where we dwell.) The Actress did many photo-shoots, she graced many magazine covers. She made this an entree to acting. I was led into films for the fun and the money. I'd loved to have kept up magazine work, but newspapers and magazines were becoming a thing of the past.

She became a great thespian, whereas I was just a ham. I worked with the same man who photographed her for the calendar that became a men's magazine cover. She needed money and posed nude for him, and would later tell the press the story of doing what was necessary to survive when broke—public sentiment went with her, instead of being judgmental over the nudity issue. I posed for "Pretty Girl" photography in the nude for my living when my high school sweetheart and I were living together in the Valley and in Hollywood. I had a couple of agents that hired me out to photographers working for the many "girly" magazines of the day. When called to work for the famous photographer one night, he took pictures of me with a whisky bottle, posing for an advertisement that would only be seen in Japan.

The photos he took of Sweetness would be sold to become the first issue of a men's magazine that continues to be published. I ended up being in the slick magazine four times, and was proud of the photos taken! It is a magazine known for beautiful women and fascinating articles, stories, jokes, comics and interviews.

She and I both posed for the painter Earl Moran. He was painting in Hollywood when my mother worked in Hollywood as a key-punch operator for the Studios. The artist took snapshots of me that he would use as ideas for a full-length painting of me that would be hung above a bar. My favorite part of my career was being photographed; it brought back good memories of my childhood with Dad. In the early days I posed nude and suggestive, but never showing any "bits." Sweetness's first job was at a plant making war supplies: the beginning of her career. The beginning of her modeling career would lead into an acting career. A photographer came to the plant to take pictures of the young ladies who worked there. Sweetness posed for him in her work overalls. The photos were printed in the army's magazines.

Modeling

She took to the camera right away, she loved to pose and saw it as a way to become an actress. Writing her husband overseas where he'd been posted, she asked for a divorce. She felt that he didn't understand her dreams and didn't seem able to encourage them. During the day she worked at the defense plant, but would pose at night for photographers at their studios. She'd pose in front of her mirror, always trying to come up with perfect looks, new poses. She ended up on a lot of magazine covers once the editors figured out that she looked great in bathing suits. She took her agent's advice, and had her brown curly hair dyed lighter and straightened for a shampoo print advertisement.

She was everywhere via the magazine covers. Even I could go to a newsstand and see a couple of magazines showing my face. People wanted to know who she was, who was this beauty in a bathing suit?

Chapter 5

Film

SWEETNESS SO LONGED to be a good Actress, wanted to be more than just a print model, wanted to prove herself on the moving screen. Acting was everything to her, it was her dream. She quit the Studio when they were insisting she make a film obviously created for a "sex-pot." She felt forced into accepting roles that were beneath her ability.

At first the Studio wasn't putting her in any films, they employed many starlets and she was just one of many. It was her fans that made a difference, and she would always love the public for "creating" her. Early print-work publicity caused much ado, and the fans wrote in to the Studio asking when they would see her in a movie. I made movies and didn't really know how famous I'd gotten until well after when attending Conventions—the fans would line up wanting a photo, wishing to thank me for my revolutionary efforts, telling me I helped to liberate them sexually. Now through social media I've made friends and fans from all over the planet! fans gather to hear me reading from my books, and they boost my ego. A hot girl needs a fan!

Fans adored her: a town actually had its name changed to hers for the day of her big Premiere.

Fans can be a blessing and a curse. A Fan of mine considered himself my Slave—that of course ended horribly! I didn't want a slave! (Though I'm frequently in need of help.) One of her fans took advantage of having met her only once: he ate off his stories for years, especially after she died! He claimed to have married her (untrue!) Fans can fantasize about stars, they can stalk and harass and cause real harm. Stars have needed to take them to court, get restraining orders.

Dumbness and sexual availability went with the breathy, childish voice she used in her films, and in interviews gave the impression that what she said was innocent and not rehearsed. The Actress started out as a pin-up model so her body was on display, and clothing played an important factor: she wore white and revealing outfits. It has been said that the way she walked was because she cut her shoes: one of her heels lower than the other. She became the American Dream, a girl who had risen from a miserable childhood to Hollywood stardom. Her screen persona was a dim-witted but sexual blonde, fans and critics believed it to be her real personality. This became difficult for her when she wanted to pursue other kinds of roles, dramatic roles. The dumb blonde was a role—she was an Actress, for heaven's sake! Such a good Actress that few believed she was anything but what she portrayed on screen.

She was well-read, continued to study, even took some classes at college in the evening. In fact, she obtained the role in a big movie because she impressed the producer with a book she was reading. She and the producer talked about the book and she sent him a copy.

Another actress and Sweetness were roommates for a time. The woman said that Sweetness loved to have fun, laughed and joked around, was fun to be with.

Acting is full of rejections—auditions can be brutal and you can feel like a piece of meat; other people judge you on your look, your hair, your weight and how tall you are—anything but your acting. There is much rejection trying to get roles for most actors. But Sweetness had a contract with a Studio; a major one-up on most players. She was rejected by just about everyone in her life, however.

Showing more of her acting range, she was able to play a fish cannery worker. To prepare, she spent time in a real fish cannery. Taking a summer school class in oceanography, I toured a tuna canning factory with my class. The smell hit you before you were even indoors, it permeated clothes like smoke. The Actress received positive reviews for her performance; one critic saying that she deserved starring-role status from then on—but when next she did star in a dramatic role, it received mixed reviews, people weren't expecting her to be so creepy, unhinged.

Other films she appeared in continued to focus on her sex appeal. One starring role was solely to present her in two bathing suits, according to its writer; she also played a secretary and a prostitute.

My acting in films was all about sex, and I never kidded myself that it was anything else. I looked on it as a lark, a way to be pleasured. For me, acting never got in the way of a hot sex scene! I did learn a little about the subject and methods of sex!

The "Father of Method Acting" first gave her private lessons; then she enrolled in his school. At first she dressed down and wore a scarf, wishing to draw no attention to herself. The teacher insisted she have therapy to be able to dig deep within herself to Act. She ended up being part of the teacher's family unit, taking trips with them and eating dinner with them. He would be left most of The Actress's estate, and her estate money would end up going to his third wife. The teacher had a daughter, an actress, and she and Sweetness became friends, like sisters. The teacher's wife, acting coach for Sweetness, became co-dependent. The Actress needing acceptance by someone close to her, she and this second coach were inseparable.

Sweetness got a reputation for being difficult on the set, and it got worse the more famous she'd get. Often late, sometimes she didn't even show up on the set. She did not remember her lines, and would want several re-takes before she was okay with her performance. Her dependence on her acting coaches irritated directors; her perfectionism, taking drugs and mental illness took their toll. She became terrified of doing anything wrong. I've always prided myself on being a "Trooper" and swore I'd never walked off a set—until, that is, I heard Howie Gordon read from his autobiography "Hindsight." The bit he wrote about me in his book tells about me walking off a set! What he says is accurate, but I'd been blocking it from my memory. So I guess I can relate to The Actress's absences—at the time of my walk-off I felt absolutely justified.

When first taking acting lessons she lived at the hotel on Hollywood Blvd. that I was in front of when I was told Elvis had died, a pivotal point of my life—one of the days the music died. Clearly I remember standing in front of the hotel's entrance doors on the pavement where the stars are embedded in the sidewalk. I remember exactly where I was sitting when we had a moment of silence (at lunch on the benches in elementary school) for the shooting death of a presidential candidate. Sweetness would meet him—rumors raged about the two of them, some of which Sweetness started.

She met an older gentleman who helped her financially. She was young and so desperately wanted to be in the movies. He helped her more than anybody; really loved the girl. He wanted her to marry him but she wouldn't, knowing it wouldn't be fair to him as she wasn't *in* love with him, although she loved him as her friend. He took her everywhere, got her auditions and told her if she married him she'd be rich when he died. She didn't want to be a "gold-digger" and refused him repeatedly. Sweetness was the protégé of this man who was then the vice president of a big modeling agency. He, as her agent, represented her and their relationship became sexual, and he proposed marriage. He paid for silicone to be implanted in her jaw and maybe for a rhinoplasty, and arranged a bit part in a comedy brothers' film. When he did die she threw herself down, crying for hours. The Actress loved this first agent in a way that a friend would love another. She had fun with him and was grateful to him and devastated when he left her. So many would leave her. But death was final and she made a big scene at his coffin, sobbing and carrying on.

Her agent and man who loved her told her she was a Star. Even when she didn't believe in herself he helped her to smile. Her first film break was because of him: she had a small role in an excellent film directed by a top man. She really liked working for this director, he seemed most interested in the actor's acting. (Some director's want to be complimented for their direction of the actor's acting.) The audiences of this film took notice of her, whistling in the theaters. Her friend the agent believed in her, told her she was broke because she was a Star, and Stars didn't get "eating money" roles—they were meant for starring roles. Sweetness wasn't able to really fall in love with the agent, but he was kind and patient. Wanting to marry her, he'd propose, but said he would wait until she was ready. He told her he had a heart condition and that she'd be rich if he died when they were married. Which was true, but she couldn't bring herself to marriage without being totally in love, felt that it just wasn't fair to him. She really liked him, he knew more about her than anyone, she was his friend and he was a very dear friend to her. He wanted to help her to achieve Stardom—her Destiny. But two Studios rejected her because she "wasn't photogenic." My True Love Paul says that you can't judge a person how they appear naturally, you must judge how they look in photographs and on film to determine if they are photogenic or not!

It was a rumor that got her a screen test. The rumor was that Howard Hughes was interested in signing her; no one knows who started the rumor. An actor-turned-talent-scout managed to sneak her in to the Studio early in the morning to do a screen test. He had acted with her Aunt's Idol in a film when he made his living as an actor. Sweetness didn't say anything on film, just moved across the room in a beautiful gown. She knew that if the Studio Head got back in town and didn't like the screen test, both the talent scout and the camera operator might get fired. The Studio Chief did like the test, however, and awarded her a contract. Auntie was her legal guardian and she signed it. It was suggested that the girl change her name, and her Aunt said she could use her mother's maiden name. It was written in the contract that the underage girl save her money. She bought a fine quality gray wool skirt that she wore several times a week with different sweaters. Every night she'd set her hair in pin curls and sleep with a hair net.

When Sweetness was first with the Studio, a director asked her what she was reading between takes. She was enthused about the writings of Lincoln Steffens, he wrote of the hardships of being poor. The director asked her not to rave about this man's work, that bad things could happen to her. Later, when she wrote down the greatest people in the world for the Studio publicity department, Lincoln Steffens was at the top of her list, but they said to take his name off—that she would be misunderstood. The writer was frowned upon because he was at the Russian Revolution, and considered a Communist. Later he saw the mistakes of the Doctrine, but his name was still linked to it. Steffens had grown up in the house in Sacramento that is now the Governor's Mansion! So she knew a little politics through reading; later her writer husband would be caught up in the fever of the panel on Un-American Activities. She was always pro Civil Rights, and when she was asked to a dinner party with an elected official, she wrote notes of questions to ask him. Her own ancestry showed that she was related to a President of the USA. My own shows that the story my dad told of his grandmother being raped by a Swede was correct, I have just that amount of Swedish blood!

The budding Actress had an acting coach at the Studio. The coach would go to all the sets where she worked. The film directors didn't like this, but her coach gave Sweetness confidence. She'd run over and over lines with the starlet until both felt the acting was perfect. Sweetness wanted perfection; they stayed up all night together getting lines just right. Sweetness auditioned for one of the top directors and he said she got the role after her first reading, but she wanted to do it over again. Because The Actress was a perfectionist she felt her coach needed to be on set to tell The Actress what she was doing wrong. The Actress paid the coach from her own pocket money and the Studio paid her as well. When The Actress tried to commit suicide, at least twice before she was nineteen—her coach got her to a hospital.

When Sweetness again took an overdose when she was twenty-four years old, bipolar disorder was determined to be the root of the problem. This reminded me that I'd too had (sort of) attempted suicide as a teenager. Once I swallowed a bottle of aspirin but it just upset my stomach, another time I took some barbiturates—only a couple, and they just made me sleep. When forty years old, I would injure myself badly and went into a month-long coma, finding no other solution to a love triangle.

During the shooting of one film, the production was delayed by The Actress's frequent absences and by the fact she and her co-star were having an affair. This affair was widely reported in the news and even used in the film's publicity! For many movies I was living with my co-star Jamie Gillis. This was written about in magazines of the day, and we got work as a couple. He even got my daily rate raised. I'd also had flings with other men and women that I worked with, but my first husband and Jamie were the long-lasting relationships during my modeling/film career. She and the French actor became friends as he was scared of looking foolish on camera, and she was insecure. He hardly knew any English, and she felt she could teach him. They both were married to famous people and she felt they had things in common.

Film

When she told the Studio bosses she'd posed for nude pictures, they were not pleased. She had been broke at the time she said, and told that to the public. Sympathy was with her, and increased interest in her. Her reputation as a new sex symbol increased even more when a columnist wrote that she usually wore no underwear! I never wore underwear until I met my last husband. He convinced me I was wearing out my jeans by doing this, and that we wouldn't need to visit the laundromat so often if I'd put on some panties. It's a major process to bag up clothes to haul up the mountain, walk to the car on the road, and drive downtown to do laundry! Paul and I love our cabin in the woods, but it has disadvantages that go with the great view. I never have worn a bra, can't stand the restriction. Though in order to really fit well into a nice dress, I will wear breast support so that my cleavage is pronounced.

The Studio worked her on back-to-back films. No time to rest, let alone rehearse. She'd get burned out and get sinus or bronchial infections. But the Studio wouldn't believe her, thought she was faking, or being lazy. The man that sat in the head office at her Studio hated Sweetness, called her dumb.

Her whole career seemed like a masculine phenomenon. She seemed to irritate women from the time she was about fourteen. They'd ignore her and talk about her "dangerous character." As a teenager I was told I was a slut, and didn't even know what the word meant. I've never worn bras because they were uncomfortable and all the girls hated me but the boys made out with me. I had a bad reputation before I'd ever done anything "bad."

One director Sweetness did a film with was known throughout the industry as a bully. His bad reputation and Sweetness did not get on! She didn't even like the project much, but she did like the songs she would sing, and had a long-time friend who co-starred. She twisted her ankle quite badly while filming one day, and wore bandages and walked with crutches due to the injury. Some people thought this was just her revenge on the bully director. I was bullied something awful by a woman director. She was generally nasty to people, made everyone work long, long hours and relentlessly did take after take when her actors were sweaty with exhaustion. The last thing we were interested in was sex, and yet we were made to perform under the harshness of this director.

Film

Sweetness had people around her to "protect" her. For instance: her acting coaches—both women became much more than mere coaches, they became infatuated with her and lived their lives around her. I've relied on my three Bills to shield me from the big world. At the time I was making films with sex they were illegal, and I was put in jail for making them. As a teenager I couldn't make friends with my own gender, and have felt girl-friendless my entire life. I do now have really great friends: some made after I retired from "The Business," some made through the internet, some made through my love Paul. My entire career as a porn star seemed to be catering to the male. Now, times have changed; I believe that the public has become more open-minded regarding sex. Recently I've discovered that I do have female fans, and "couple" fans. I've met them at book signings and Conventions, when interviewed—wonderful people I've had much pleasure meeting. Most importantly, I've discovered the deeper layers of my being, the "Artist Self."

I shot a film in 3-D: originally called *Disco Dolls in 3-D*. This working title changed to *Blonde Emmanuelle*. Fun film—especially for Bill Margold who played the villain; he chewed up the scenery. I was filmed in an open car with helicopters carrying camera-people shooting me. There were even some "civilians" watching from the dunes. I got to wear my favorite black and silver gown through most of the movie—slipping it off and on again.

The first "big hit" of Sweetness's career was originally shot with the new process of 3-D. But the Studio saw how very good the film was, and decided to release it without the extra gimmick. Her co-star in the movie was another gorgeous woman (with dark brown hair) who was very kind to Sweetness. She'd pop by to see The Actress each morning with an encouraging word, a friendly hello. Sweetness was thrilled to be given this plum role, and had singing and dancing coaches to enhance her part. Because of her contract with the Studio, she was given much, much, much less money (tens of thousands less) than her co-star. She and her brunette co-star put their handprints and signed their names in cement on Hollywood Blvd.—her dream as a girl coming true. She really didn't care about money, all she ever wanted was to be wonderful and have a happy life. She owned a car, wore beautiful clothes and furs, all she missed was having a child. What she wanted on this set was her own dressing room, for which she actually fought with the Studio! She was their Star! In fact, the Head of the Studio wouldn't believe Sweetness had done her own singing in the Big Hit, until she marched into his office and sang! During the making of this film she not only got her own dressing room, but the Studio Head changed his mind about her—from detesting her to becoming a supporter. I hope that I've changed peoples' minds about me: I hope they can look past the porn star image to accepting me as an Artist. Like her, I can be sexy, but I'm also smart, talented and have feelings.

She always had the same hair and make-up people that worked on her for her movie roles. I knew Gordon Bau quite well, he'd worked on many films, including *Shoot-Out at Medicine Bend* with Angie Dickinson and Randolph Scott. (Angie was a known lover of President Kennedy, and Randolph lived with Cary Grant—who enjoyed dropping LSD.) I'd go to Gordon's home and he'd tell me about movie stars that he'd known. He was developing a line of pancake make-up. We had a lot of fun visiting, until a couple moved in with him. The man and woman started taking over his life—answering his phone, not letting him eat what he wanted, taking his money. They were mean to him and rude to me; they made it known that they'd like it if I left. They were more strange every time I'd go to Gordon's house in the hills of Hollywood. The last time I went to visit, they'd tied Gordon to a dining chair! I was already in the house, so I visited as if nothing was amiss—but when the couple left the room I quickly jumped out a window! Running, falling, I made my way to a neighbor's to call the police.

I was "discovered" at the Bob's Big Boy where I worked in Toluca Lake—by a make-up artist whose father worked on the *Get Smart* TV show. And the make-up artist that gave me the "Serena" look was David Clark, who I adored. Sweetness also developed a Look, and could roam New York City undetected if not wearing make-up.

After years on the East Coast she moved back to California. She dated the Italian/American Singer again and purchased a house, going to Mexico to buy furnishings. She went to work again for the Studio, yet would be absent from the set of her last (unfinished) film because of illness. It was a re-make, and would star Sweetness and another Italian/American friend of hers who was a singer-and-actor. Just before filming began, she caught a disease of her sinuses. Doctors warned the Studio to postpone, but they would not and proceeded on schedule. The Studio even leaked that their Star was faking illness!

She did take time off to fly to the East Coast once to sing for her friend in office, calling attention to herself with the flesh-colored dress she literally was sewn into! The Studio had not wanted her to go.

The press was invited by the Studio to take photographs of the scene where Sweetness was nude in a swimming pool. But when Sweetness was again sick they fired her! And sued her! And replaced her! The co-star singer-and-actor protested and declared that he would not work with anyone but Sweetness. The Studio sued him too, and the film was shut down. Then they'd initiated a negative publicity campaign, saying that she was mentally disturbed and the cause of the film's shutdown. It wasn't long before they regretted losing her and made a new contract including a starring role in another film. Sweetness had been doing her own publicity by posing for major magazines, including the top fashion magazine.

Sweetness continued to play a part in the creation of her public image, and towards the end had almost complete control. She made friends with gossip writers and had final say over photographs released of her. She was compared to her Actress Idol, and even hired the Idol's hairdresser to dye her hair.

I've seen all her films, of course. Always sexy, yet you can see her comic genius. The dramatic roles she played were of an insane person and a murdering wife—she was absolutely believable.

Perhaps just to avoid Sweetness's by now well-known "dis-temper," her co-stars were nice to her. I was friendly to the folks I worked with, I felt it made the long days of filming more pleasant, maybe even feel like they went faster. I was especially considerate of the movie crew—they could make me beautiful with the placement of lights, placement of the camera. And although I would have sex with the other actors, we would rarely become friends—it was just a job! We were just going through the motions. Jamie Gillis was the one to break the rule: We were friends and lovers and worked with one another. My life with Jamie was one big fat sex scene: on and off camera. He was gentle while being rough, so I was able to walk after our sex play!

Directors make all the difference to a film as they make all the on-set decisions. They can make or break a performer by praising or being critical of their acting abilities. Directors have the ultimate power on what goes on their set; they could throw Sweetness into fits of uncertainly, followed by tears and/or lateness. I worked with the great Howard Ziehm, who was known to me from his break-out film *Flesh Gordon*, and he was careful with my ego. I had such a great time shooting for him that I agreed to be in three of his films, some of my best film work.

Pictorial Interlude

Photo by Paul Johnston

Photo by Paul Johnston

Pictorial Interlude

Photo by R.A. Morgan

Photo by Kenji

Photo by Steve Zambrano

Photo by Steve Zambrano

Photo by Steve Zambrano

Photo by Steve Zambrano

Photo by Steve Zambrano

Pictorial Interlude

Photo by Kenji

Photo by Kenji

Photo by Kenji

Photo by Kenji

Photo by Baron Wolman

Pictorial Interlude

Photo by Baron Wolman

Photo by Baron Wolman

PICTORIAL INTERLUDE

Photo by Baron Wolman

Photo by Baron Wolman

Pictorial Interlude

Photo by Baron Wolman

Photo by Steve Zambrano

Chapter 6

First Husbands

SWEETNESS SAYS LIFE was miserable until the boys began to notice how she was growing. She'd wrestle with them on the beach and give them a kiss on the cheek. Once her breasts appeared she began making friends—all boys, they'd ask to walk her home and carry her books. My biggest tip serving food was from a table of men wanting to see me walk away!

When I developed titties, my mature life of Sex and Porn and Exploration began. Sweetness developed early and looked old for her age and was "married off." (I also looked older than I was and was able to lie about my age to enter establishments with alcohol, for instance.)

She got pushed into a marriage with the boy next door. I married my childhood sweetheart; neither of our marriages would work—too young, we knew nothing and wanted the world.

She was divorced and living in a room in Hollywood by the time she was nineteen. At that age I was busy with my baby daughter.

She had Love affairs, I had affairs. My longest-lasting was with Jamie Gillis, the Prince of Porn. (My friend John Holmes being the undisputed King.) She also had love affairs with co-stars. I felt true to my first husband in heart, but was anything but faithful to him with my body. I wasn't being satisfied sexually at home, so doing porno would be highly beneficial to my sanity.

My heart was broken by the disaster of my first marriage. When I first started making movies I would only work with my first husband—it was my way of being loyal to him, but he didn't care and was tempted by all the other women on the set. First husband has never cut his hair, it's his freak flag—but to work with me he'd wear short wigs. Even with all the outer rebellion of my life, I feel I'm old-fashioned, even conservative in some aspects: Mom and Dad raised me right! He was my first real love, my puppy-love. I cried over him for years, missed him, mourned over our parting. Even when with others, I'd think of him. Yet he and I were not meant to be—we didn't get along at all. I wanted it to work, but my heart was foolish and still young. Sweetness married while underage, it seemed the best of choices for her. While I was active sexually, she didn't know much as a teenager. She didn't know how to cook, whereas if I had brown rice I could prepare a feast. She was so proud that one of her "Aunts" made her wedding dress, and that they all attended the ceremony. I got married in black velvet, driven to the courthouse in a hearse, with no witnesses in attendance. I should have gotten the symbology. I've learned to watch for omens.

I remember being sent home once early in my modeling career. The man and woman photographers were unhappy with the condition in which I showed up. Because of the fights between my first husband and me, my eyes were red from crying and my eye make-up streaked. I was an emotional mess, but showed up to the gig because I was desperate for money. They couldn't have used me, I know now—I was a disaster.

I was very immature when married the first time. I didn't know what love was, and was extremely jealous of my husband. I'd stalk him, attacking women with whom he'd speak, attack him at home and in public. I was jealous of every minute that he wasn't showering attention upon me. I couldn't stand it when we were apart, hated that he'd spend any time with anyone else. I was completely wrong but needed time to learn this. I had a lot of growing up to do. I see now that jealousy in my case stemmed from very low self-esteem—and I just wasn't his type.

She was faithful to her first husband, only because of her lack of desire for sex. She didn't understand sex; she was too young, still quite childlike. Her Aunt married her off at age sixteen. She really didn't know much about the sex act beyond "fooling around," was scared to death of what her new husband would do to her. She was happy that another "Aunt" designed her wedding gown and that both her Aunts attended her wedding. Her husband later said she was a good wife overall, but she couldn't cook. What she liked to do was play with the neighborhood kids on the island, until her husband called her home in the evening. I recall playing ball in our street until my dad whistled for me to come to dinner.

Her husband was posted to Catalina Island and she went with him. She thought it was fun living there, but didn't like the fact that her husband was jealous. There were a lot of men stationed there: Sailors and Marines who'd whistle. But she was always faithful to her husband. When he went to Shanghai, she went back to mainland California to be with his family, and the future Model/Actress got a job in a plant that made things for the war effort. It was there she was discovered by a photographer.

I am a native Californian but didn't visit Catalina until I was married to my True Love Paul; he'd never been there either. After the book opening of *25 Golden Goddesses* by Jill C. Nelson (a photo of me with my hair red is the cover image) we went to vacation. He and I took a ship from Long Beach to go to the island, staying a few days. We walked around a lot, hiked, loved our trip. He and I both love architecture and the houses there are very interesting to us, the gardens plentiful. I had my hair done by a young woman who'd never left the island. Paul and

I ate at a fancy restaurant and had croissants and muffins every morning at our posh hotel next to the ocean. We had a wonderful time and hope to return some day, perhaps to see the buffalo herd on the other side of the island. The bison were left there after they were used for a movie, and have thrived.

When famous, Sweetness made an appearance by joining a party by arriving by helicopter. I arrived in a helicopter for my role opposite Marilyn Chambers in *Insatiable*. I also went to "The Land" by helicopter to attempt to serve custody papers on my first husband. He spoke with his rifle and I heard a bullet whiz past my cheek. I had done this per my lawyer's advice. After this I ended up in court for years, hiring a total of three lawyers. (One named her child Serena after me!)

My daughter grew up without me, her real (biological) mother. Unfortunately, her father and I fought like the proverbial cats and dogs, and he found my untreated bipolar affliction too much to handle. Because we had no idea what was happening to me, he was scared of me, of the way I'd act when "possessed" by my demon disease. We were poor, not insured, and neither of us even thought of going to a doctor. Not that a doctor might have understood—I was misdiagnosed until I was twenty-seven. My Baby-Daddy ran off with her into the hills and I was left to go to court to get custody. When my daughter turned of age, she (out of curiosity, I'm sure) came back into my life. It took time for us to get to know one another, but discovered we were alike in so many ways, even liking the same old movies. She has always been the diamond in my eye, the reason my eyes sparkle—and we've grown to love and rely on each other. She also has an actress as an Idol, although my daughter's favorite was Sweetness's competition at the Studio. I applaud my daughter's choice. Her favorite actress was a real fighter, and did much for the understanding of AIDS (which was the reason I stopped filming) and raised money for AIDS research.

Chapter 7

Second Husbands

THE ACTRESS AND HER COACH lived together for a time. But soon The Actress felt the coach was becoming too possessive, felt that she acted too much like a spouse. Yet another great director banned the coach from his set. Sweetness continued daily training with the acting coach, but studied elsewhere also. Sweetness was a perfectionist—often taking several takes to get a scene just right. The coach was banned from four film sets, and she didn't get along with Sweetness's second husband. By then our girl had grown into a Star.

Sweetness had heard the Sports Star's name, but she didn't even know if he played football or baseball. (He was enormously famous.) The Sports Star and Sweetness argued about the way she dressed, and she ended up wearing clothes that buttoned all the way up and had collars. She'd been wearing publicity-seeking low-necklines. Bosoms were what got men aroused then, today butts are big (literally)—fashions change. I've never had an abundance of either; I made do with dressing in garter-belts and using my seductive mouth. The Sports Star always avoided the press, even when playing ball. I've used publicity to help sell my paintings and books. Thanks to being a model and having acted in X-rated films, I've been able to reach the public.

During my second marriage, I went through waves of super-manic behavior. He did attempt to help me retrieve my own daughter and I wept each day for her. His money spurred on my mania with spending, shopping. I did shop until I dropped from exhaustion. I shopped all his money and much more, running up numerous credit accounts. I had checkbooks and never added or subtracted the money, so never knew have much I had—though I was usually deep in a hole. I didn't want to know how much I had, I was fever-pitched, running scared and doing a self-soothing by spending someone else's money. I felt neglected due to the fact he spent all his time on the phone making money. I had free access to the money, but not to him. He'd only need me to perform sexually with other people to satisfy his voyeur needs—I felt used and not loved, but loved my big flashy diamond ring. Always overdrawn in both my life and my checkbook, I was spinning away from my true nature towards a hard crash. Writing more and more bad checks, there was no money to cover them—I borrowed from credit cards and kept applying for more. Running in manic glee and horror, running the cards up to the limit. Faster and faster I'd spend, buying worthless things I didn't want, things I'd give away to my family or charity or never use. It was the act of buying that filled me—just for that moment. The fulfillment would never last, so I was on a constant search to become whole and happy. My disease was untreated, not diagnosed until I was nearly thirty years old.

I've heard that Sweetness was probably also bipolar, that would accountant for many of her actions. I wasn't diagnosed properly for the first part of my life. It took much experimentation with medications to balance my emotions. I took and then stopped taking many anti-depressants, gained and lost many pounds. Ballooned up and was fat on these drugs. I've always taken this statement of her condition with a grain of salt—there were many stories of why she was what she was. But when I read recently that she owed money when she died I thought perhaps she did have trouble with money management as I did due to being bipolar. It was reported that she was worth so much money, and I believed that—but she had been borrowing heavily to stay afloat, spending tremendous amounts that she didn't have and was actually overdrawn at the bank! Yet the public would be told that she had a lot of money. Millions would be made by her Estate throughout the years to come, her money going to someone she never knew when alive.

With my second husband in the deluxe surroundings of The Olympic Tower in Manhattan, I'd scream and cry in bed with the pain of the scar tissue in my ovarian tubes. I berated myself while I sobbed, "You have nothing to be sad over—look around you! You are in a beautiful apartment in the sky!" But my pain would lead me into depression. I just stayed in bed, miserable; the pain was always mixed up with my deep dark moods. And while living in a condo set at the water's edge in Coconut Grove, Florida I'd be in bed crying. Not enjoying the sparkling blue bay or sunshine above because I was either depressed or in pain, or depressed because I was in pain. It was here, finally, at the age of twenty-seven, that I was recognized as being bipolar. And it was there at Mercy Hospital I had my insides out—had to get rid of all of it, I was precancerous. Although I would have liked to have more children, my body wasn't up to that task—and I've never been sorry that menstruation went away!

She had surgery for her endometriosis, had a cholecystectomy. Sweetness was in the hospital for a month. She was put in a psychiatric ward (for depression) against her will. Her new friend, her ex-husband the Sports Star, helped her get out of that place.

She and a heart-throb Singer became friends and lovers; she loved his voice. He gave her front row seats to his sold-out concerts. The Singer was another Italian American. He and the Sports Star were buddies. Sweetness befriended an Italian woman working for her in New York living with her third husband and another Italian/American would co-star in her last, unfinished, movie.

The Star Athlete showed he was jealous of her once they married. He even hired detectives to follow her—after they were separated! He and the Singer ended up breaking into a ladies apartment one night, believing Sweetness was there. The Actress was in the building, but they broke into the wrong place! The woman in the apartment that was broken into ended up suing the men. Sports Star couldn't seem to let go, but Sweetness did count on his friendship when married to her next husband, a famous writer.

Sweetness was typecast. However, she knew that this was an act. She wanted to change her public image: she longed for other kinds of roles, and to be respected in her business. The biggest untruth about her was that she was dumb and couldn't act. She read well-regarded literature; the dumb blonde was a role—she was an Actress. The character Sweetness created and lived in like a body-mask was an Archetype.

The Sports Star she married wanted a good Italian wife, one who would take care of him in retirement. But Sweetness grew tired of watching TV every night. I am never bored doing the same thing day after day with the Man I Love, I've had sufficient excitement in my life! The Sports Star would talk sports with men, and sometimes didn't talk to Sweetness for days. She never learned the rules of baseball, but had fun at the stadium watching games. He didn't know his own strength, he did hurt her physically. She never felt that he meant to hurt her. Her make-up artist noticed marks on her face and managed to cover the bruises so no one would know. She told people that she that was biting herself when sleeping.

Posing for photographers in New York City got her in trouble at home with the Sports Star. The revealing photos that she posed for were the excuse her husband gave for divorce. The film was shot in Hollywood but the Studio decided to generate publicity featuring a subway grate, which became one of her most famous scenes. While shooting, many gathered to watch; her husband was full of jealousy. The divorce was after only nine months of marriage.

She was unable to escape her Fame. (As Lady Gaga named it: the "Fame Monster.") In NYC she went out incognito by wearing scarves, or a wig, no make-up. She could take off the "mask" of her film persona. In California she was hounded by the press, though she was able to make good use of what they'd say. When I retired from my X-rated film career I left the life completely—it was even reported via the internet that I'd died! No one that knew me heard from me, I was busy with a second marriage and a full-time painting career. I disappeared for twenty years into my studio. I did get in touch with Bill Margold after I'd come out of a coma. To help retrieve my lost memory I wrote what I could remember of my life story. Bill was always kind to me, like my own brother; he would write the Forward to my book "Bright Lights, Lonely Nights." After so many years of being gone from "The Biz" I have met new friends: Annie Sprinkle and Beth are my bestest, and I adore Christy Canyon and a relative newcomer called Cannibal. (The latter being like the child of Bill Margold: he always said that if he and I were to have a child she would be Cannibal.)

Sweetness had a stepson with the Sports Star, and they loved each other very much. I had stepkids when I married the artist, and though our relationship was rocky his kids and I loved each other a lot. Even years after I'd lived with them they call me Mommy Serena. Sweetness had many phone calls from her stepson after she and his father had broken up—the young man relied on her advice as he would a mother's counsel. In fact, the evening of the night she died they spoke on the phone about a problem he was having. I made good friends with my in-laws when I married the publicist—I watched them both die, I was there. His mother was like a mother to me, but mostly a great friend. We'd have a long lunch with her every Saturday, and she and I would have our nails and hair done together, chatting about our week. It's always good to have family, even someone else's family. Make your own family.

During her honeymoon with the Sports Star the newspaper applauded him as a great hero, and called her his butt-swinging wife. Crowds cheered wherever they went and she was thrilled with the noise they made; he'd heard it before in stadiums when he played with his team. She ended up leaving him about a year after marriage because their goals were so different. He was retired, she on her way up. He was old-fashioned, wanted a stay-at-home wife; she played that as a "role" briefly, but got bored. However, after being divorced and becoming close again as friends, rumors were spreading that they might get back together romantically. He helped pick out a woman to care for Sweetness's institutionalized mother, and the woman would play the role of a spy for him at The Actress's house. This woman would go over The Actress's private papers after she died, she would burn many of Sweetness's letters and papers in front of The Actress's half-sister!

The Sports Star was already retired, she was on the way up the Hollywood ladder. Still married to the Sports Star, she had a lover who was convinced that her big black Cadillac was bugged. When in NYC, she started to carry a change-purse to use the coins for public telephones. (Anybody remember telephone booths?) She may have been paranoid, but her phones were bugged and her rooms WERE bugged.

My second marriage, like hers, was a time to retire from public life. I was thrilled to be out of the grind of fame and films, while she was not at all ready to lie low as her husband the Sports Star would have preferred. I happily moved onto another career: that of painting and exhibiting and selling my art works. She was meant for the screen and could not be fulfilled by any other activity. I was able to become known as an artist. Painting was therapy for my jangled brain, I could completely escape outward stress. The stress of fame: being on display, being crowded by other's expectations. I was able to get grounded and find myself, find the quiet places of contemplation by secluding myself in the art studio, preparing myself for the Hermit's Life of my True Love.

Chapter 8

Third Husbands

ALTHOUGH SWEETNESS BECAME one of the Studio's biggest stars, her contract had not changed, meaning that she was paid less than other stars of her stature and could not choose her roles in projects. The Head of the Studio made it known that he disliked her and did not think she would earn the Studio much if she was in dramas. She refused to begin an inane musical.

Trying to get control over her career she ended up leaving Tinsel-Town. She'd met a photographer who offered her a home in which to stay with him and his wife. A home located across the country. They'd form their own production company. She thought that she was no longer under contract to the Studio but was mistaken, and a legal battle went on. A film was made with a big-breasted blonde who played a dumb actress who starts her own production company!

When in NYC she had her name legally changed to the one she'd been using, the name the Studio and her Aunt had given her. She talked about that part of herself as "Her," a mask, an aura she could put on. As a teenybopper I had an alias: "Shannon." I loved this name and used it when talking to policemen and when hitchhiking. Sometimes my girlfriend and I would each use our fake names to one another, and make up personalities. My One True Love has "Shannon" in his family tree—both as first and last names!

Sweetness was caught in the middle of two men who loved her, The Athlete she was married to, and The Author who was married to someone else! I was married at the time I fell in love with Paul, and that break-up reconstructed my life, and deeply hurt my husband—he still stalks me. But I could do nothing but go where the Love was. The Actress begged The Author not to get a divorce because of her. I was glad for my divorce because I could see no other path open to me; I would give up everything to follow Paul. While she became a Jew to marry The Author, I became a Jew and tried to bring my second husband back to the faith. Busha had always told our family there was a rabbi in our line way-back-when, and my mom and I gravitated towards Judaism. I became a Re-constructionist Jew, which is "left" of Reform. My rabbi taught his own form of thought, heavily influenced by his years of studying Zen and Hinduism. I had grown up going to a Vedanta Temple, so I was very comfortable going to services on Friday nights with Rabbi Rami Shapiro.

My True Love and I have been together now over twenty years and hope for at least twenty more. It's so easy living with him, though I know I can be "High Maintenance." Thank you, Darling, for putting up with all my annoying ways. I tell him everyday how very much I love him, he *shows* me how much he cares. Her third husband seemed distant to her, but he was absent from her because he was writing about her!

For the first production of her own company she went overseas as a newlywed with the writer.

The film didn't go well. The male star of the film decided he should direct, and he instantly hated the acting coach Sweetness brought along. The wife of this actor/director was slipping more and more into her insanity, so he was between two very fragile, difficult women. Sweetness wasn't at all happy on the set because she felt that he talked down to her. The root of their problem was that he was a classically trained actor, she'd been taught Method Acting. On this film in England, she was late most days, but never more than about an hour late. She needed to wear the hat of both Actress and Producer.

During the production of this film, Sweetness and The Writer had to move several times to get away from the press and her legion of fans. They still found out where Sweetness lived, and would hide in the bushes and by the gates of their estate. They were loaned a manor by a Lord and his wife for the duration of filming. When Sweetness took a weekend off to be with her new husband, the foreign press grew angry with her and wrote untruths about her, they wanted access to her and could be spiteful.

People that knew her away from film sets knew her to be nice—reserved but friendly, polite. Well deserving my nickname for her: "Sweetness". She'd behave as a normal person, not like a Star at all. People knew her as a regular person, not as the most famous woman on earth! Of course I've never experienced such fame, very few have. Never have scores of fans surrounded me, just to get a glimpse. I've lived a simple life, indulging in silences and peace. (The only time I had scores of kids follow me was in NYC when living with Jamie Gillis. The young men there adored Jamie—they were actually following him!)

She stayed close to the stepchildren she had. One of the children I helped learn to read still calls me Mommy Serena. I just saw a neighbor kid I'd considered a little sister, and she told me she considered me a second mother. She's all grown up now with four children in college, and I'll always love her like my own blood. I've also adopted "nephews," grown men and newborns! If they need me I'll be there for them.

The famous Writer was in his room writing a good deal of the time—wouldn't even come out for dinner, so The Actress spent most of her time with the seamstress, who proved to be good company. When I lived in San Francisco I made my roommate friends into sex-partners, a photographer and a cook. The photographer (whom I loved, will always love) would become my daughter's "Manny" and the cook would become an X-rated film Star!

The Star of Literature looked like Abraham Lincoln to her; she was a great fan of the President. She agreed with the Writer's politics, and loved the fact that he was tall. There was a bad omen on the day she married the Writer, however. The reporters that were following the couple had a car crash and one of them died. Sweetness felt it was another bad omen that they lived on the thirteenth floor in NYC. At their apartment she was left alone with her friend the seamstress a lot—her husband seemed to be in his office writing all the time. The Actress wouldn't go out without her husband on her arm, but he (like the Sports Star) never wanted to go out.

The Writer got caught up in politics and had to testify before the House on Un-American Activities. He had indeed gone to Communist gatherings. Sweetness stood by him. When that public fight ended, she began to plan a modern house on a hill on property he owned. She wanted her home designed by the most controversial architect of the time.

She wanted to have a baby so badly, she wanted company, someone to care for, and hoped it would bring her marriage together. She was pregnant during the filming of her comedy shot in beautiful black and white, but lost that baby. She really thought that a baby would have solved all the problems in her marriage. Though my first marriage wouldn't end well, we do share a wonderful daughter.

The Writer began to write a film script for The Actress. The writing took years, and The Actress felt that he loved her when he started, but hated her by the time he finished. He was still writing on the set while they filmed; she thought that the finished product wasn't that great of a script. The Actress did get to work with the actor she'd always thought looked like the photograph of her father. The director and her husband rewrote the script every night, so The Actress never knew what to expect on the set. She moved into another bedroom while filming the movie so that her husband could write at night. She was given noontime calls on this shoot, which still felt too early for her. She got violently ill with abdominal pains—they were so bad that she couldn't eat.

The actor who starred with her in this film looked like the man she thought was her father. He was so kind to her on the movie set *and* had been in several movies with the Actress Idol that Aunt had styled her after. But Sweetness was miserable because her husband the Writer was making her crazy and the desert heat was too much.

This was the last film The Actress completed, the one that her husband had written to provide her with a dramatic role. The filming in remote deserts between July and November was difficult. The four-year marriage of The Actress and the Writer was over, and he took up with a still-photographer on the set. Sweetness didn't like the fact that he had based her role partly on her life, and thought it inferior to the men's roles. She struggled every day with reading the lines she was supposed to say. Her health was failing due to the pain of gallstones. Her drug addiction was so severe that her make-up had to be applied while she was still asleep. Shooting was halted in late summer so that she could spend a week at a hospital, drying out.

The Writer was an intellectual, a thinker. He was a complicated man, and his feelings for The Actress began and ended with Guilt. He felt guilt-pangs over being attracted to her while still married, felt guilty over leaving his wife and children. Then when his marriage to Sweetness faltered he felt guilty for not being able to "save" her. He kept a private diary of his feelings about her, which she would get at and read. These private thoughts that he'd written down hurt her and she knew then it was over between them. He wrote in his diary that he no longer loved her and Sweetness never trusted him again. I write frequently in my journal, but wouldn't want my mate to read it—I write about our fights, and don't mean what I rant when angry.

The script he wrote for her turned into a disaster—during filming the heat of the desert would make her ill, and as a finished film it was a flop. The Writer had a good idea, but the director also thought he could write. Between the two men she was in a state of confusion—being given the lines the morning they would shoot film.

For him it had a happy ending because he ended up making one of the crew members his girlfriend. But to Sweetness this last movie she'd ever make felt bad; she felt bad, thinking for a time that she'd caused the leading man's heart attack that killed him. He was the actor she'd always thought that her father looked like, so this would have been a terrible blow to her. Luckily his wife had a long talk with her, and assured Sweetness she had nothing to do with it.

During shooting of the film she was often late, not knowing her lines. She'd say she'd be on the set, yet would worry the hours away in her dressing room. Sometimes she'd insist on forty "takes," yet other times she'd be word-perfect. A co-star asked the director how many times were they going to do a scene over and over, and the director wisely answered "As many times as it takes to satisfy her." She was something special, her comedic genius unparalleled for someone who learned to act as she went. When she was satisfied with her performance, that's when the set could be wrapped.

When the Writer married again after he and Sweetness divorced, the new wife had a baby, which upset Sweetness. She'd always feel "less than" because she couldn't bear children. After hearing the news of the birth, Sweetness again took an overdose of pills and needed her stomach pumped. When I threw myself off that mountain I ended up in a month-long coma. After that I dreamed of throwing myself off the Golden Gate Bridge. During the time of my healing, my man has helped me realize that I would hurt many people if I was to kill myself. He has taught me how to love, to realize that I have much to live for. He's taught me to respect myself and to remember to honor the Gift of Life. I no longer dream of the bridge.

The Actress wouldn't be seen out at the Hollywood parties except in the beginning when she was "climbing;" she preferred the company of a few friends at home. I don't go out much, although I had my Disco period when that was hot—Jamie and I would close down the dance clubs in New York. Now I only go out to eat on special occasions. Rare that you find my True Love and I out after dark. We stay in to make dinner (he's a great cook!) and watch television or movies. I will be on the computer, paint or hook rugs while listening to TV, movies or music. The Actress didn't watch

TV, unless there was a movie on, or something she wanted to hear about on the news. She liked the fact that people were going out to the movie theaters, because it would get folks out of their houses.

Chapter 9

Drugs & Drugs

HAVING TO WORK for the foster families of her youth, she was used to it: the directors on her first few films all noted her work ethic. She'd scrubbed floors in order to eat. She worked very hard learning song and dance numbers, and usually only needed one take. She learned the technical side of film-making. I too learned: While in Florida I made my living as a photographer.

It was the Fame Monster that ended up killing Sweetness. The more famous she became, the more unsure she was of herself and the more drugs she'd take. The more famous she became, the more hangers-on would hang on, the more the Studio would use her and exhaust her, the more drugs she'd take, the less sleep she'd get—the more drugs she'd take. Poor girl, people felt sorry for her, then grew annoyed with her lateness, and she'd take more drugs. People would forgive her because of her stellar performances, but they'd be irritated and appalled by her behavior. She didn't even own much, everything loaned to her by the Studio—the Studio would make millions. One gown she'd worn in a film was later bought at auction for over one million dollars!

Sweetness had a good friend from the days when she was starting out modeling, a newspaper writer. He was perhaps the first to give her illegal drugs; he was an addict himself, that's why he hung out at a fabled pharmacy.

She had a sadness in her eyes that even a smile couldn't mask. Her breathless, baby voice drew you in to her sorrow, wanting to smooth her way and make her well. One could not fill what drugs and sadness made. I did drugs and reached the depths of depression and soul-sickness and poverty because of them. I found good drugs as well, and saw amazing things and had merry times.

Drugs & Drugs

That's one of the drawbacks of drug taking—you're always hoping for a good high. In the end I needed to rid myself of the poison of drugs, most are a one-way street to nowhere. Luckily, now, in a more enlightened time, marijuana has become widespread and (mostly) legal. It is just a weed, a living plant.

What I found to be "bad" drugs if done to excess: uppers and downers, body drugs. Drugs to keep her awake and to help her sleep—are what undid Sweetness. She got so addicted there was no turning back for her. Addiction claimed another life. Like Judy Garland, Elvis Presley and Janis Joplin overdoing drugs (and not being able to stop), drugs would kill her.

The singer/actor who worked with her on the film that was never completed knew her before she'd gotten screwed up by drugs. He said that she was very sweet when younger, but on this last film she was all illusion, that there was nothing alive behind her eyes.

I read the autobiography of the actor who'd marry into the government family. Sweetness knew him and his wife, who was part of that big Irish family. Sweetness would visit them at their waterfront beach house. Reading about his life, I learned he was heavily addicted to alcohol and Sweetness would drink with him. He got so drunk at his daughter's wedding that he didn't even remember being there! Part of me understands why he drank; he was drowning the memory of a truly horrid mother and upbringing. There was a time I drank in excess, I can sympathize.

As she did more drugs, she became known as difficult. Always late, insecure, demanding perfection. Sweetness never meant to be late, exactly. She get lost in thoughts and daydreams taking long, long baths—then take hours to apply creams and lotions. If she became too late she'd feel so guilty that she wouldn't show up at all. She was insecure her whole life—always expecting everything to be taken from her, never completely trusting most people.

At the top of her fame she wasn't able to save money, she was living paycheck to paycheck. I never made much, what I did earn went to my husband for weed, or directly up my nose. Cocaine was a Demon Drug, seemingly everywhere in the 1970s. The powder didn't get you high, just kept you buzzed, awake. It burned holes through your nostrils and burned holes in your wallet. Thank the goddess I put an end to that!

People in the Arts would regularly be given sleeping pills in the 1950s and 1960s. The Rolling Stones would call such pills "Mother's Little Helper." They were prescribed to many before being seen as addictive. Actors loved them because they'd sleep heavily and be able to look good in the morning. A problem that Sweetness had was taking them with a great amount of champagne and misinformation. People with mental issues turn to drugs to "self-medicate." I used wine that way for years, but now that my levels are level I can drink or not drink—it is now my choice rather than a feverish compulsion. The reason I drank has been taken care of, so now instead of needing drink to feel better I can enjoy a sip. While doctors first were having me test different combinations of drugs, I assumed I was an alcoholic and stopped drinking for years.

She knew some politics, through her husbands, by reading, by being introduced to political figures, and by asking questions. She told friends she was dating men in high office, one of the reasons there was so much rumor regarding her death. Conspiracy theories abounded with both the Mafia and the Government accused.

The night that she died was her "nurse"/housekeeper/spy's last day to work for Sweetness—so why was she there spending the night (???) Her actor friend with the beach house got a call from Sweetness saying goodbye. She was slurring her words so he panicked and started calling people to check on her. He was advised not to go himself because his in-laws were politically famous, and a scandal would hurt them. Her friend the actor called for hours, he was extremely worried. Sweetness was proved to be already dead when her housekeeper took the calls and told people that Sweetness was fine (???). Between the doctor who cared for Sweetness and the housekeeper who spied for him many untruths were told about that night. Both stated they used a fireplace poker to push aside the curtain is Sweetness's bedroom—but this was impossible because The Actress stapled the black-out curtain to the wall. I had those heavy curtains in NYC, but the city's constant hum would still keep me up. Even now I sleep under the covers to shield me from any light, and luckily it's quiet here in the woods. The doctor and the housekeeper didn't call the police for at least four hours (???) after they found Sweetness dead.

The films I have made are well in my past—something I did as a raving/ranting bipolar person. I've never regretted what I did, I have nothing to apologize for, I am proud of who I am and how I got here. I am no longer that person, but because of my films I have a public persona and am able to sell books I write and the artwork I make. Sweetness also was what the directors and her roles made her—and more. I understand her because I too was not the person I pretended to be on set. I was happy on set because my sexual needs were filled—at home I was mostly sad. And I drank too much. I did take illegal drugs at that time. Doctors prescribed for Sweetness, but because she'd go to more than one doctor, she was taking more than her limit.

She felt that she was being followed. I know what it's like to feel the many eyes watching through the lens. It is true that a government agency did keep a file on her, as well as the men with government jobs with whom she associated. The first time she met one of the men in a high-ranking government position, she was excited and told friends she'd be going on a date with him. This was another of her stories; she was invited to a dinner party that the man and his wife also attended. I have been allowed to live (much to my surprise after all the drugs I took "back in the day") after throwing myself off a mountain. I have found the Partner of my Dreams, a man who completes me—and I've found contentment in my Art. Writing poems and books of my experiences, I have new fans of this work; I have been able to use my small fame to grow a full life as an Artist, Activist and Author. Animal lover—people are animals too!

Sweetness was never allowed the space to develop, she so wanted to be known as a true Actress, capable of portraying any role.

She had so much that she was looking forward to, including a book she was writing with an old friend. He was a photographer, and when she was suspended by the Studio they shot photos on the beach. She didn't work for the Studio for quite a time, they waged a press war against her, and sued her! The film company fired her for all her missed days on the set, they refused to believe she was sick. While doing the photos for the book with her friend, Sweetness played in the surf like a kid, happy.

Another photographer friend was seeing a psychiatrist, and so she also started going to visit her. Both the psychiatrist and this photographer would give The Actress pills to sleep. She had so much trouble sleeping at night; she'd take some pills and still would need more. The Actress loved to sleep, all day if possible. She wanted to have sweet dreams so that life wouldn't bother her.

The make-up man that applied make-up on her in her coffin also worked on her when she was too tired to awaken from drug stupors. He did her make-up when she was asleep. She could swallow a handful of barbiturates without water. The more drugs she took, the more paranoid The Actress became. She was hooked on medication to sleep, needing more and more. She took very heavy drugs, and when doctors would prescribe only so many pills, she just shopped for another doctor. Doctors were happy to have a Star patient. There were fifteen bottles of drugs next to her bed. In the end she'd been dating the Italian Singer again, but he grew weary of her making drunken/drugged scenes. She even began shooting up drugs from a vial she carried, saying it was her "Vitamin Shot." In the bottle was a mixture of three drugs, and when she'd take a shot of it she wasn't much good for anything but sleep. People around her described her as "glazed"—her gaze was glazed over but she'd say everything was just fine.

Each book I've read about The Actress tells a part of the truth. I've tried to soak up facts about her, and am sifting them through my own vision. I am not an expert on her, I never met her (wonder if I'd even want to!) but have loved her deeply as my Idol and as a teacher of what is good, and what not to do. Each book I read ended up the same, with her death of an overdose of drugs. The next reading of a book about her was more difficult to get through for me; each book I read I'd dread how it ended: I wished to save Sweetness, to warn her to turn away from certain people and situations that would lead her to drugs. Years passed in which every time I'd attempt to get through a book about The Actress I'd end up sobbing while reading. I'd get so forlorn I'd need to stop my inquiry of her, I just couldn't take the pain it was giving me. I'd set aside my writing for long periods as I just couldn't handle my aching for her—I was just too involved. Sweetness is not only an Idol to me, but a sorrow to me. Seeing her in movies I love her acting, her happiness, but also know the backstage struggles that got her to the film. Her life is there over every thought I have of her: each time she makes me laugh I cry inwardly a little.

I too have insomnia and have taken many drugs to knock me out. I write down my dreams, but night terrors seem to have been vanquished. When having nightmares, I'd wake up drenched with sweat, waking up to the sound of my own screaming. That all has subsided once I got my serotonin levels balanced, which I do with carefully prescribed chemicals. Now, I've finally found what works to "level me out" thanks to my nurse practitioner Carrie really listening to me. Doctors must listen so that the diagnosis is right, the medication correct. I take minimum amounts of medications to help my bipolar, my insomnia, my low thyroid, my anxiety. I have a terrible time getting to sleep; sometimes I never do get to sleep at night, though I usually can cat-nap in the afternoon. (Aren't cats smart?) Sweetness also had trouble sleeping, so I do understand taking drugs (because I do too) to help her sleep. She would keep upping the dosage, which is not a good thing; and drinking, not a good mixture. She never had proper medical care. So-called friends would give her medications, and shrinks would prescribe medicine as well. Delving into her past didn't help her, I believe. Too much living in the past is burdensome.

With the combination of perfectionism, low self-esteem, stage fright, anxiety, and chronic insomnia, she began to use more barbiturates, amphetamines, and drink alcohol. Of course using these medications exaggerated her problems—a "viscious circle" as my mother would say.

For years her death remained a mystery—could it have been suicide, accidental suicide, or even murder? A re-investigation opened decades after her death—because of the widespread, still growing rumors—concluded that the finding of accidental suicide stood. However, she always said she was being spied upon—she wasn't sure—it could have been the Government, maybe her ex-husband. Was it the Mafia through her friend the singer's contacts, even the political personages with whom she was acquainted? Her house was found to have bugging equipment all over it! The wiring was so secret that it wasn't found until her house had sold and the roof replaced!

Her death was front page news worldwide. It seemed so sudden, and she had so much to look forward to. Many have concocted theories as to the actual events. Many, including myself, do not think it was suicide. One opinion is that her housekeeper/spy was there that night and gave Sweetness an enema with too many drugs in it—maybe. Sweetness often did this, and she was also planning to fire the woman. I've also had to take enemas, heavy drugs will leave you unable to go to the bathroom. Now I just drink psyllium.

The housekeeper, who falsely claimed to be a nurse, was there, and says she woke up in the middle of the night feeling something was wrong (???). When there was no response at The Actress's door, she called the psychiatrist. He broke a window and found Sweetness dead in her bed. Then her MD was called who pronounced her deceased, then the police were called. Plenty of time to stage the scene. Her doctors said she had overdosed several times, and her death was officially deemed a probable suicide.

It has been said that the suicide rate in Los Angeles doubled the month after she died. Her death was blamed on her fame and the way people spied on her. One of her directors said she was "one of the most unappreciated people in the world." Her funeral was private and attended by only those closest to her, though hundreds were in the streets around the cemetery. The service was put on by the Sports Star and he refused attendance to anyone who was in show business.

Sweetness was looking forward to many great changes in her life. Among the bottles of drugs (and prescriptions for more) littering her floor and nightstand when she died:

A telegram offering new work.

Afterword

LIFE IS SHORT, ART LONG.

I've taken my "Stay at Home" order to use my time to finish this book. Though I usually am at home, creating something, this Covid-19 pandemic has forced me to think about what I need to accomplish with my life.

This book is a Project I really wanted to see finished. I reached out to all my friends, fans and family to see if anyone would be interested in helping me with it. And the adage "ask and you shall receive" certainly worked—again! All you need to do is be sure of what you want, then ask for it; the

Universe will provide. I've trusted in this all my life, because it works! The right person has come back into my life and is assisting me with this book. I've thought of him through many years of separation, and it's like a miracle to have him back in my life. I am so thankful to know him, to be with my Paul, and to be alive! So thankful for what little talent comes through me.

I take walks wearing a mask, wash my hands, try to not touch my face, have gotten tested. People paid for the entire town of Bolinas to be tested—how incredibly generous. Many thanks.

I am blessed to be born white, middle class and to live in California, though as a woman I still don't have full and equal rights under the law.

California is a Nation-State, forged by seekers. I loved San Francisco mayor Gavin Newsom as my Mayor, and admire him even more as our Governor. I thank him for taking it slow concerning this pandemic.

It is worldwide, and needs to be taken very seriously. Thoughout the ages people have been killed off by other plagues, I have hope of surviving this one. If not, I hope that my Art will endure.

Afterword

Quarantine-while, our abused planet is getting a break from pollution, the birds seem to be singing louder because the din has lessened. My hope is that people might see how clear the rivers and canals, and be more respectful of our Mother. Our Fearful Leader, I call him "Agent Orange," wants his fake economy back and the people back in churches where they infect one another. I know he doesn't get that he'd be killing only people that might vote for him. I fear for our Democracy.

Agent Orange wants to be a king, and it seems that he is following the rule book of Dictators. I hope that "bad" people get second chances and can become good people. I pray, for the good of the planet and for all the good people to live as one.

Now there has been rioting due to the racist environment we exist in. I am all for Peaceful Protests, it's our right as good American citizens—our duty to help make change. The incident that has caused this latest unrest is the torture to death of George Floyd. This act, caught on video, should warrant a "First Degree Murder by Torture" charge. I can but hope that things will change for the better and that

ALL men will be equal—isn't that in the Constitution? Our country was formed on the backs of enslaved people.

Black Lives Matter.

Peace.